Scalable Software Architecture Patterns for Serverless Systems

No more wasting money on idle servers. Architecting for Agility, Efficiency, and Limitless Growth. Learn how to build systems that are not just scalable, but superbly efficient.

Katie Millie

Scalable Software Architecture Patterns for Serverless Systems

No more wasting money on idle servers. Architecting for Agility, Efficiency, and Limitless Growth. Learn how to build systems that are not just scalable, but superbly efficient.

By

Katie Millie

Copyright notice

Copyright © 2024 Katie Millie. All Rights Reserved.

Welcome to the enchanting realm of Katie Millie, where boundless creativity intertwines with cutting-edge innovation! This material, a true reflection of Katie Millie's distinct vision, is safeguarded under copyright law. Unauthorized use, reproduction, or distribution is strictly forbidden and will be subject to legal action.

At Katie Millie, we champion the power of imagination and the wonder of originality. Every piece of content is a testament to countless hours of meticulous dedication, boundless creativity, and unwavering passion. Be it a captivating story, a stunning design, or a soulful melody, each creation is crafted with utmost care and precision to inspire and enchant.

By accessing or utilizing this material, you agree to honor the immense effort and intellectual property invested by Katie Millie.

Thank you for accompanying us on Katie Millie's creative journey. Together, let us continue to explore uncharted territories, innovate fearlessly, and dream without limits!

Table of Contents

INTRODUCTION

Chapter 1

    The Scalability Imperative: Why Serverless Matters in the Age of Big Data

        The Power of Patterns: Building Scalable Systems with Confidence

            A Roadmap for Success: What You'll Learn in This Book

Chapter 2

    Understanding Scalability: Vertical vs. Horizontal Scaling

        Bottlenecks in Traditional Architectures: When Scaling Becomes Painful

            The Rise of Serverless: A New Paradigm for Scalable Applications

Chapter 3

    Unveiling Serverless Architecture: Core Concepts and Benefits

        Event-Driven Communication: Building Loosely Coupled Systems

            Advantages of Serverless: Automatic Scaling, Cost Efficiency, and Agility

Chapter 4

    Stateless Function Principles: Avoiding State Management for Scalability

        Decomposing Workflows into Smaller, Independent Functions

            Handling Long-Running Processes:

Asynchronous Workflows and Queues

Chapter 5
Event-Driven Scalability: Orchestrating Services with Asynchronous Messaging

Designing Scalable Event Pipelines: Producers, Consumers, and Error Handling

Implementing Fan-Out and Fan-In Patterns for Increased Throughput

Chapter 6
Microservices for Scalability and Maintainability: Breaking Down the Monolithic

Serverless Microservices: Leveraging the Benefits of Both Approaches

Designing Microservices Boundaries for Scalability and Loose Coupling

Chapter 7
Understanding Caching: Optimizing Performance and Reducing Costs

Implementing Caching at the Edge and Application Layers

Invalidation Strategies: Keeping Caches Fresh and Consistent

Chapter 8
Asynchronous Workflows and Queues: Handling Long-Running Processes

Choosing the Right Queueing System for Your Needs: Managed vs. Self-Hosted

Implementing Retries and Dead-Lettering for Robustness in Serverless Systems

Chapter 9
Scaling for High Traffic: Techniques for Handling

- Peak Loads
  - Auto-Scaling Techniques: Dynamically Adjusting Resources Based on Demand
    - Handling Cold Starts: Optimizing Function Startup Times
- Chapter 10
  - Serverless Cost Optimization Strategies: Building Efficient Systems
    - Monitoring and Analyzing Costs: Identifying Areas for Improvement in Serverless Systems
      - Right-Sizing Resources: Choosing the Right Function Type and Memory Allocation
- Chapter 11
  - Security Best Practices for Serverless: Authentication, Authorization, and Encryption
    - Securing APIs and Functions: Protecting Your Endpoints and Data
      - Compliance Considerations: Building Secure Serverless Systems for Regulated Industries
- Chapter 12
  - Serverless on the Edge: Bringing Computing Closer to the Data
    - Serverless Machine Learning: Leveraging Serverless for AI/ML Workloads
      - Continuous Integration and Delivery (CI/CD) for Serverless Systems
- Conclusion
  - Appendix
    - Glossary of Serverless Terms
      - Serverless Best Practices Checklist

INTRODUCTION

Scalable Software Architecture Patterns for Serverless Systems: Break the Chains, Unleash Limitless Growth

Imagine a world where your applications scale effortlessly, handling surges in traffic like a seasoned surfer riding a monster wave. Costs plummet, freeing up resources for innovation, and agility becomes your middle name. This isn't science fiction; it's the electrifying reality of serverless systems – a paradigm shift that's rewriting the rules of software architecture.

But here's the catch: navigating this uncharted territory requires a map, a compass, and a deep understanding of how to build systems that thrive, not just survive. **Scalable Software Architecture Patterns for Serverless Systems** is your comprehensive guide, your battle cry for conquering the scalability challenge in the age of big data.

Forget the days of wrestling with monolithic applications, constantly battling scaling bottlenecks. Traditional architectures often buckle under pressure, leaving you scrambling to provision more servers, manage complex infrastructure, and frantically optimizing code to squeeze out the last drop of performance. Serverless flips the script, offering a revolutionary approach:

- **Effortless Scaling:** Say goodbye to manual scaling headaches. Serverless systems

automatically adjust resources based on demand, scaling up seamlessly to handle peak loads and scaling back down to save costs during idle periods. Imagine never having to worry about server capacity again!
- **Unmatched Agility:** Forget months-long development cycles. Serverless empowers you to build applications with incredible speed and agility. Focus on crafting innovative features, not infrastructure management, and deploy updates with lightning-fast speed. Innovation becomes your new superpower.
- **Cost Efficiency Unleashed:** Serverless is a pay-per-use model, meaning you only pay for the resources your application actually consumes. No more wasting money on idle servers. Serverless helps you optimize your bottom line while delivering exceptional performance.

This book is more than just a theoretical exploration. It's a battle-tested guide, packed with practical patterns and real-world war stories. You'll discover:

- **The Art of Stateless Functions:** Craft functions that are lightweight, independent, and scale effortlessly. Eliminate state management headaches and unleash the full potential of serverless.
- **Event-Driven Scalability:** Master the art of asynchronous communication, the language of serverless. Orchestrate services with events,

allowing your system to react and evolve with the flow of data.
- **Microservices for the Win:** Break down monolithic applications into bite-sized, highly scalable microservices. Leverage the benefits of both microservices and serverless for ultimate agility and maintainability.
- **Advanced Optimization Techniques:** Explore caching strategies, asynchronous workflows, and best practices for handling peak traffic. Learn how to build systems that are not just scalable, but superbly efficient.
- **Cost Optimization Strategies:** Become a serverless cost ninja! Delve into techniques for minimizing resource consumption and analyzing costs for continuous improvement.

Scalable Software Architecture Patterns for Serverless Systems doesn't just equip you with the knowledge to build scalable applications; it empowers you to build for the future. We'll explore emerging trends like serverless on the edge and serverless machine learning, giving you a glimpse into the ever-evolving serverless landscape.

Are you ready to break free from the shackles of traditional architecture and build applications that scale with your ambition? Dive into this book, unlock the power of serverless patterns, and watch your projects soar to new heights. The future of software development is scalable, agile, and serverless. Are you in?

Chapter 1

The Scalability Imperative: Why Serverless Matters in the Age of Big Data

In today's digital landscape, characterized by the relentless growth of data, businesses are constantly seeking ways to efficiently manage, process, and derive insights from vast amounts of information. The age of Big Data presents unique challenges and opportunities, making scalability a critical requirement for modern software architectures. Serverless computing has emerged as a pivotal paradigm, addressing these scalability needs with remarkable efficiency and cost-effectiveness. This essay explores the scalability imperative in the context of Big Data and elucidates why serverless architecture is increasingly becoming the go-to solution for enterprises navigating this complex terrain.

The Scalability Challenge in Big Data

Big Data refers to extremely large datasets that may be structured, semi-structured, or unstructured, and that are generated at high velocity from diverse sources. Traditional data processing frameworks struggle under the weight of such voluminous data, often leading to bottlenecks and inefficiencies. Scalability, in this context, implies the ability of a system to handle a growing amount of work or its potential to accommodate growth. For Big Data applications, this means efficiently processing massive datasets, dynamically adjusting to workload changes, and maintaining performance levels without exorbitant costs.

Serverless Computing: A Scalable Solution

Serverless computing, also known as Function-as-a-Service (FaaS), abstracts the underlying infrastructure, allowing developers to focus solely on writing code. In a serverless model, the cloud provider automatically manages the infrastructure, scaling resources up or down in response to the application's needs. This automatic scaling is particularly beneficial for Big Data applications, which often experience unpredictable and highly variable workloads.

Key Benefits of Serverless for Big Data Scalability

1. Automatic Scaling: Serverless platforms such as AWS Lambda, Google Cloud Functions, and Azure Functions automatically scale to handle spikes in data processing tasks. This is crucial for Big Data applications, where data influx can be erratic and substantial. Automatic scaling ensures that computational resources are dynamically allocated based on current demand, optimizing performance and cost-efficiency.

2. Cost Efficiency: In a serverless architecture, users pay only for the actual compute time used, rather than provisioning and paying for fixed resources. This pay-as-you-go model is highly advantageous in Big Data scenarios, where processing requirements can vary significantly. It eliminates the need for over-provisioning and reduces costs associated with idle resources.

3. Event-Driven Processing: Serverless architectures are inherently event-driven, making them ideal for Big Data workflows that require real-time processing. For instance, serverless functions can be triggered by data streams, changes in a database, or external events, enabling real-time data analytics and processing pipelines.

4. Microservices Architecture: Serverless aligns well with microservices, where applications are composed of small, independent services that communicate over well-defined APIs. This modular approach enhances scalability, as each function can independently scale and manage its workload. For Big Data applications, this means different parts of the data processing pipeline can be scaled individually, optimizing resource usage.

Scalable Software Architecture Patterns in Serverless Systems

To leverage the full potential of serverless for Big Data, certain architectural patterns are particularly effective:

1. Data Lake Architecture: Combining serverless functions with data lakes allows for scalable ingestion, storage, and processing of vast datasets. Serverless functions can preprocess and transform incoming data before it lands in the data lake, enabling efficient downstream analytics.

2. Stream Processing: Serverless functions can process data streams in real-time, handling tasks like data transformation, filtering, and aggregation. This pattern is crucial for applications requiring immediate insights from continuous data flows, such as IoT analytics or financial transaction monitoring.

3. Orchestration and Workflow Automation: Serverless workflows, managed through services like AWS Step Functions or Azure Durable Functions, enable the orchestration of complex data processing pipelines. These workflows can scale individual steps based on workload, ensuring efficient and reliable execution of end-to-end data processes.

In the age of Big Data, scalability is not merely an option but a necessity. Serverless computing offers a powerful paradigm to meet this scalability imperative, providing automatic scaling, cost efficiency, and robust handling of real-time and event-driven workloads. By adopting scalable software architecture patterns in serverless systems, organizations can harness the full potential of Big Data, driving innovation and gaining a competitive edge in an increasingly data-driven world.

The Power of Patterns: Building Scalable Systems with Confidence

In an era where digital transformation drives business success, the demand for scalable, resilient, and efficient software systems is paramount. Serverless computing has emerged as a transformative approach, offering unparalleled scalability and flexibility. Central to harnessing the full potential of serverless architectures are scalable software architecture patterns. These patterns provide a blueprint for building robust systems that can confidently handle varying workloads and complex operations. This essay explores the power of these patterns in constructing scalable systems within the realm of serverless computing.

Understanding Serverless Computing

Serverless computing, or Function-as-a-Service (FaaS), abstracts the underlying infrastructure, allowing developers to focus on code while cloud providers manage servers, scaling, and maintenance. This paradigm shifts the operational burden from developers to the cloud provider, enabling rapid development and deployment of applications. Serverless architectures inherently support automatic scaling, event-driven execution, and a pay-per-use model, making them ideal for modern applications that require flexibility and efficiency.

The Importance of Architectural Patterns

Architectural patterns are tried-and-tested solutions to common design challenges. In the context of serverless systems, these patterns encapsulate best practices for achieving scalability, reliability, and maintainability. By leveraging these patterns, developers can build systems with confidence, knowing that their solutions are robust and scalable.

Key Scalable Software Architecture Patterns for Serverless Systems

1. Microservices Architecture

Microservices architecture decomposes an application into small, loosely coupled services, each responsible for a specific business capability. This modularity enhances scalability as each service can be independently deployed and scaled. In a serverless environment, microservices are implemented as individual serverless functions that interact over well-defined APIs. This approach ensures that different parts of the system can scale independently based on demand, optimizing resource usage and performance.

2. Event-Driven Architecture

Event-driven architecture is a natural fit for serverless systems. In this pattern, components communicate through events, which are generated in response to changes or actions within the system. Serverless functions are triggered by these events, enabling real-time processing and decoupling of components. This pattern is especially useful for applications with high variability in workloads, such as e-commerce platforms or IoT applications, where real-time responsiveness is crucial.

3. Data Lake Architecture

Data lakes are centralized repositories that store raw data in its native format until needed for analysis. Combining serverless functions with a data lake architecture facilitates scalable data ingestion, storage, and processing. Serverless functions can preprocess and transform data as it arrives, ensuring that the data lake remains organized and ready for analytical queries. This pattern supports scalable Big Data processing and analytics, making it invaluable for organizations dealing with large volumes of diverse data.

4. CQRS (Command Query Responsibility Segregation)

CQRS is a pattern that separates the handling of read and write operations. In serverless architectures, this separation can be achieved by using different serverless functions for commands (writes) and queries (reads). This allows for independent scaling of read and write workloads, improving performance and scalability. CQRS is particularly beneficial for applications with complex data interactions and high read/write throughput, such as financial systems or social media platforms.

5. Saga Pattern

The Saga pattern is used to manage distributed transactions in microservices architectures. In serverless systems, it orchestrates a sequence of local transactions across multiple serverless functions, ensuring data consistency and recovery from failures. This pattern is crucial for maintaining consistency in systems where transactions span multiple services, such as e-commerce order processing

Building with Confidence

The true power of these scalable software architecture patterns lies in their ability to instill confidence in developers. By adhering to proven design principles, developers can anticipate and mitigate potential issues, ensuring that their systems can gracefully handle scale, complexity, and change. These patterns provide a roadmap for constructing serverless systems that are not only scalable but also resilient and maintainable.

In the fast-evolving digital landscape, building scalable systems with confidence is a critical imperative. Serverless computing, coupled with robust architectural patterns, offers a powerful framework for achieving this goal. By leveraging patterns such as microservices, event-driven architecture, data lakes, CQRS, and the Saga pattern, developers can design and deploy systems that are prepared to handle the demands of modern applications. These patterns empower organizations to innovate rapidly, respond to changing requirements, and harness the full potential of their data, driving success in a competitive marketplace.

A Roadmap for Success: What You'll Learn in This Book

In the rapidly evolving world of software development, the ability to build scalable, resilient, and efficient systems is a critical skill. As organizations increasingly adopt serverless computing to manage dynamic workloads and complex applications, understanding scalable software architecture patterns becomes paramount. This book serves as a comprehensive guide, offering you the knowledge and tools needed to master serverless architectures and implement scalable solutions with confidence. Here's a roadmap of what you'll learn as you journey through this book.

Introduction to Serverless Computing

We begin with an introduction to the serverless paradigm, explaining what serverless computing is and why it has become a game-changer in modern software development. You'll learn about the core principles of serverless, including its event-driven nature, automatic scaling capabilities, and the pay-per-use pricing model. This foundation will set the stage for exploring how serverless architectures can be leveraged to build scalable systems.

The Importance of Scalability

Next, we delve into the concept of scalability and its significance in today's data-driven world. You'll gain an understanding of the challenges associated with scaling traditional systems and how serverless computing addresses these challenges. This section will highlight the importance of designing systems that can gracefully handle increasing loads and varying workloads without compromising performance or cost-efficiency.

Key Architectural Patterns for Scalability

This book covers a range of architectural patterns that are essential for building scalable serverless systems. Each pattern is discussed in detail, with practical examples and use cases to illustrate its application.

Microservices Architecture

You'll learn how to decompose monolithic applications into microservices, each implemented as independent serverless functions. This section will cover best practices for designing, deploying, and managing microservices, emphasizing how this modular approach enhances scalability and flexibility.

Event-Driven Architecture

We explore the event-driven architecture pattern, which is integral to serverless systems. You'll understand how to design systems that respond to events in real-time, decoupling components and enabling asynchronous processing. This pattern is particularly useful for applications that require immediate responsiveness and can scale based on event volume.

Data Lake Architecture

This section focuses on the data lake architecture, a scalable solution for storing and analyzing vast amounts of data. You'll learn how to integrate serverless functions with data lakes to facilitate efficient data ingestion, transformation, and querying. This pattern supports scalable Big Data processing and is essential for organizations dealing with large datasets.

CQRS (Command Query Responsibility Segregation)

You'll explore the CQRS pattern, which separates read and write operations to optimize performance and scalability. This section will guide you on how to implement CQRS in serverless architectures, allowing for independent scaling of read and write workloads.

This pattern is particularly valuable for applications with high read/write throughput requirements.

Saga Pattern

The Saga pattern is crucial for managing distributed transactions in microservices architectures. You'll learn how to use this pattern in serverless systems to ensure data consistency and handle failures gracefully. This section will provide you with strategies for orchestrating complex transactions across multiple services.

Practical Implementation and Best Practices

Beyond theoretical knowledge, this book emphasizes practical implementation. You'll find step-by-step guides, code examples, and best practices for deploying serverless applications. Topics covered include designing for failure, optimizing performance, and ensuring security in serverless environments. By following these guidelines, you'll be able to build robust and scalable serverless systems.

Case Studies and Real-World Applications

To solidify your understanding, this book includes case studies and real-world applications of serverless architectures. You'll see how leading companies have successfully implemented scalable serverless solutions, overcoming challenges and achieving significant benefits. These examples will inspire and inform your own serverless projects.

Future Trends and Emerging Technologies

We conclude with a look at the future of serverless computing and emerging technologies that will shape the next generation of scalable systems. You'll gain insights into advancements in serverless platforms, new architectural patterns, and how to stay ahead in the ever-evolving landscape of software development.

By the end of this book, you'll have a deep understanding of scalable software architecture patterns for serverless systems. You'll be equipped with the knowledge and skills to design, implement, and manage serverless applications that can handle the demands of modern workloads. This roadmap for success will empower you to build scalable systems with confidence, driving innovation and excellence in your organization.

Chapter 2

Understanding Scalability: Vertical vs. Horizontal Scaling

In the realm of software architecture, scalability is the ability of a system to handle increased loads by adding resources either vertically or horizontally. Vertical scaling (scale-up) involves adding more power to existing machines (e.g., CPU, RAM), while horizontal scaling (scale-out) involves adding more machines to a system. Serverless architectures, which are inherently designed for horizontal scaling, leverage both approaches in various contexts to ensure efficient and responsive systems. This essay explores vertical and horizontal scaling, highlighting their differences, advantages, and how they integrate into scalable serverless systems.

Vertical Scaling (Scale-Up)

Vertical scaling enhances a single node's capacity by adding more CPU, RAM, or disk space. It's akin to upgrading your computer to handle more tasks simultaneously.

Advantages of Vertical Scaling

1. Simplicity: Easier to implement since it involves upgrading existing infrastructure.

2. Compatibility: Suitable for applications with strict consistency requirements or legacy systems that may not support distributed computing.

3. Reduced Complexity: Avoids the need for complex distributed systems, simplifying development and maintenance.

Disadvantages of Vertical Scaling

1. Limitations: Limited by the hardware capacity of a single machine; there's a ceiling to how much you can scale vertically.

2. Single Point of Failure: If the machine fails, the entire system goes down.

3. Cost: High-end hardware can be expensive and may not offer proportional performance gains.

Horizontal Scaling (Scale-Out)

Horizontal scaling increases system capacity by adding more nodes (servers) to a system, distributing the load across multiple machines.

Advantages of Horizontal Scaling

1. Unlimited Scalability: Theoretically unlimited, as you can keep adding nodes to handle increasing loads.

2. Redundancy and Fault Tolerance: With multiple nodes, the system can withstand node failures without significant downtime.

3. Cost-Effective: Often more cost-effective than vertical scaling as it uses commodity hardware.

Disadvantages of Horizontal Scaling

1. Complexity: Requires sophisticated load balancing, data distribution, and consistency management.

2. Latency: Increased network latency due to communication between nodes.

3. Development Overhead: Requires applications to be designed with distributed architecture principles.

Vertical vs. Horizontal Scaling in Serverless Architectures

Serverless architectures, exemplified by platforms like AWS Lambda, Google Cloud Functions, and Azure Functions, are designed for horizontal scaling. They inherently handle scaling by spinning up multiple instances of serverless functions to manage increased loads. Let's explore how serverless systems leverage these scaling approaches.

Serverless Horizontal Scaling: An Example

Consider a serverless function that processes user uploads in a photo-sharing application. When a user uploads a photo, an event triggers the serverless function to process the image (e.g., resize, add filters).

```python
import boto3
from PIL import Image
import io

s3 = boto3.client('s3')

def lambda_handler(event, context):
    # Get the uploaded image from S3
    bucket = event['Records'][0]['s3']['bucket']['name']
    key = event['Records'][0]['s3']['object']['key']

    response = s3.get_object(Bucket=bucket, Key=key)
```

```
    image = 
Image.open(io.BytesIO(response['Body'].read()))

    # Process the image (resize, filter, etc.)
    image = image.resize((100, 100))

    # Save the processed image back to S3
    buffer = io.BytesIO()
    image.save(buffer, 'JPEG')
    buffer.seek(0)

    s3.put_object(Bucket=bucket, Key=f'processed/{key}', Body=buffer)

    return {
       'statusCode': 200,
       'body': 'Image processed successfully'
    }
```

In this example, AWS Lambda automatically scales out by creating multiple instances of `lambda_handler` to handle concurrent uploads. Each instance processes a different image, ensuring the system can handle high volumes of uploads simultaneously.

Vertical Scaling in Serverless Architectures

While serverless platforms primarily focus on horizontal scaling, vertical scaling can still play a role, especially in backend services like databases. For example, Amazon RDS allows vertical scaling by increasing the instance size to handle larger databases or more intensive queries.

```sql
-- SQL command to upgrade RDS instance size
ALTER DB INSTANCE mydatabase
MODIFY DB INSTANCE CLASS db.m5.large;
```

This command increases the instance size for an RDS database, enhancing its capacity to handle more significant loads. In a serverless environment, this might be necessary for backend databases that support the serverless functions.

Combining Vertical and Horizontal Scaling

For optimal performance and cost efficiency, serverless architectures often combine vertical and horizontal scaling. Here's how:

1. Event-Driven Functions with Scalable Databases:
Serverless functions scale horizontally, processing events concurrently, while the underlying database may scale vertically to handle increased query loads.

2. Microservices Architecture: Different microservices can scale independently. For example, a user authentication service might scale vertically for robust security checks, while a content delivery service scales horizontally to handle user requests.

Architectural Patterns for Scalable Serverless Systems

To fully leverage scalability in serverless architectures, several architectural patterns are useful:

1. Microservices Architecture

Microservices break down applications into small, independent services, each with its own scaling strategy.

```python
# Example: User Authentication Service
def auth_handler(event, context):
    # Authenticate user
    ...

# Example: Content Delivery Service
def content_handler(event, context):
    # Deliver content
    ...
```

```

Each service can scale independently, optimizing resource usage and performance.

## 2. Event-Driven Architecture

Serverless functions naturally support event-driven architectures, where events trigger specific functions.

```python
# Event handling function
def event_handler(event, context):
    # Process event
    ...
```

Events can be user actions, data changes, or external triggers, and each event type can scale horizontally as needed.

3. Data Lake Architecture

A data lake architecture integrates serverless functions with scalable storage for Big Data processing.

```python
# Function to process data in a data lake

```
def data_processor(event, context):
    # Process incoming data
    ...
```

Serverless functions handle data ingestion and processing, scaling out to manage large volumes of data.

4. CQRS (Command Query Responsibility Segregation)

CQRS separates read and write operations, allowing them to scale independently.

```python
# Command (write) function
def command_handler(event, context):
    # Handle write operations
    ...

# Query (read) function
def query_handler(event, context):
    # Handle read operations
    ...
```

This separation optimizes performance for systems with high read/write demands.

5. Saga Pattern

The Saga pattern manages distributed transactions, ensuring data consistency across services.

```python
# Example saga step function
def saga_step_handler(event, context):
    # Execute transaction step
    ...
```

Serverless functions coordinate transaction steps, scaling as needed to maintain consistency.

Understanding vertical and horizontal scaling is crucial for building scalable software systems. While vertical scaling involves enhancing a single node's capacity, horizontal scaling distributes the load across multiple nodes. Serverless architectures, designed for horizontal scaling, provide automatic scaling and efficient resource management, essential for modern applications.

By leveraging architectural patterns like microservices, event-driven architecture, data lakes, CQRS, and the Saga pattern, developers can design and implement robust, scalable serverless systems. These patterns ensure that applications can handle increased loads, maintain performance, and optimize costs, empowering organizations to meet the demands of a dynamic digital landscape.

As you apply these principles and patterns, you'll be able to build scalable serverless systems with confidence, ensuring that your applications are prepared for growth and change in an ever-evolving technological environment.

Bottlenecks in Traditional Architectures: When Scaling Becomes Painful

Scaling applications efficiently is a critical requirement in today's digital landscape, where demand can fluctuate rapidly and unpredictably. Traditional architectures often struggle with scalability, leading to performance bottlenecks and inefficiencies. This essay explores the common bottlenecks in traditional architectures, how these issues make scaling painful, and how serverless systems can alleviate these challenges using scalable software architecture patterns.

Common Bottlenecks in Traditional Architectures

Traditional architectures typically follow a monolithic or tightly coupled design, where components are interdependent and run on a fixed set of resources. As load increases, these architectures encounter several bottlenecks:

1. Resource Contention

In monolithic applications, multiple processes or threads compete for limited CPU, memory, and I/O resources. This contention can lead to performance degradation, especially under high load.

Example:

```java
// Example of a monolithic application with resource contention
public class MonolithicApp {
    public static void main(String[] args) {
        // Multiple threads competing for CPU and memory
        Thread thread1 = new Thread(new Task());
        Thread thread2 = new Thread(new Task());
        thread1.start();
        thread2.start();
    }
}

class Task implements Runnable {
    @Override
    public void run() {
```

```
    // Intensive computation
    for (int i = 0; i < 1000000; i++) {
        System.out.println(i);
    }
  }
```

2. Database Bottlenecks

Traditional architectures often rely on a single relational database for all data storage and retrieval. As the number of read and write operations increases, the database becomes a bottleneck, limiting the overall scalability of the application.

Example:

```sql
-- SQL query to retrieve all users
SELECT * FROM users;
```

In high-traffic applications, such queries can lead to slow response times and database lock contention.

3. Scaling Limitations

Scaling monolithic applications typically involves vertical scaling, which means upgrading the hardware to more powerful machines. This approach has physical and cost limitations, making it unsustainable for large-scale applications.

4. Single Point of Failure

Monolithic applications often have single points of failure, meaning that if one component fails, the entire system can go down. This lack of redundancy makes the system vulnerable and less resilient.

Pain Points in Scaling Traditional Architectures

1. Complexity in Maintenance

Maintaining and updating monolithic applications becomes increasingly complex as the codebase grows. Changes in one part of the application can have unintended consequences in other parts, making development and debugging challenging.

2. Deployment Challenges

Deploying a monolithic application requires the entire application to be built, tested, and deployed as a single unit. This approach increases the risk of downtime and makes it difficult to implement continuous deployment practices.

3. Inefficient Resource Utilization

Traditional architectures often lead to inefficient resource utilization because scaling is not granular. You cannot scale individual components independently, leading to over-provisioning and increased costs.

Alleviating Bottlenecks with Serverless Architectures

Serverless computing, or Function-as-a-Service (FaaS), addresses many of the scaling challenges inherent in traditional architectures. Serverless platforms like AWS Lambda, Google Cloud Functions, and Azure Functions provide automatic scaling, event-driven execution, and pay-per-use pricing. Let's explore how serverless systems alleviate these bottlenecks using scalable software architecture patterns.

Key Scalable Software Architecture Patterns for Serverless Systems

1. Microservices Architecture

Microservices decompose a monolithic application into smaller, independent services. Each service is responsible for a specific functionality and can be developed, deployed, and scaled independently.

Example:

```python
# Example of a microservice for user authentication
def auth_handler(event, context):
    # Authenticate user
    if authenticate(event['username'], event['password']):
        return {
            'statusCode': 200,
            'body': 'Authentication successful'
        }
    else:
        return {
            'statusCode': 401,
            'body': 'Authentication failed'
        }

def authenticate(username, password):
    # Dummy authentication logic
    return username == 'admin' and password == 'password'
```

By breaking down the application into microservices, each service can be scaled independently based on its specific load, reducing resource contention and improving scalability.

2. Event-Driven Architecture

Event-driven architecture is a natural fit for serverless systems. In this pattern, components communicate through events, allowing for asynchronous processing and decoupling of components.

Example:

```python
import boto3

s3 = boto3.client('s3')

def lambda_handler(event, context):
    # Event triggered by an S3 upload
    bucket = event['Records'][0]['s3']['bucket']['name']
    key = event['Records'][0]['s3']['object']['key']

    # Process the uploaded file
    response = s3.get_object(Bucket=bucket, Key=key)
    content = response['Body'].read().decode('utf-8')

    print(f'File content: {content}')
```

```
    return {
       'statusCode': 200,
       'body': 'File processed successfully'
    }
```

In this example, an S3 event triggers a Lambda function, which processes the uploaded file. The function can scale horizontally to handle multiple events concurrently, reducing latency and improving responsiveness.

3. Data Lake Architecture

Data lakes are centralized repositories that store raw data in its native format. Combining serverless functions with data lakes allows for scalable ingestion, storage, and processing of vast datasets.

Example:

```python
import boto3

s3 = boto3.client('s3')

def data_processor(event, context):
    # Process incoming data
```

```
    for record in event['Records']:
        bucket = record['s3']['bucket']['name']
        key = record['s3']['object']['key']

        response = s3.get_object(Bucket=bucket, Key=key)
        data = response['Body'].read().decode('utf-8')

        # Perform data transformation
        transformed_data = transform_data(data)

        # Store transformed data
        s3.put_object(Bucket='processed-data-bucket', Key=key, Body=transformed_data)

    return {
        'statusCode': 200,
        'body': 'Data processed successfully'
    }

def transform_data(data):
    # Example data transformation
    return data.upper()
```

Serverless functions handle data processing tasks, scaling out to manage large volumes of data efficiently. This approach is essential for organizations dealing with Big Data.

4. CQRS (Command Query Responsibility Segregation)

CQRS separates read and write operations, allowing them to scale independently. This pattern is particularly useful for applications with high read/write throughput requirements.

Example:

```python
# Command (write) function
def command_handler(event, context):
    # Handle write operations
    save_to_database(event['data'])
    return {
        'statusCode': 200,
        'body': 'Write operation successful'
    }

# Query (read) function
def query_handler(event, context):
    # Handle read operations
    data = read_from_database(event['query'])
    return {
        'statusCode': 200,
        'body': data
```

```
    }

def save_to_database(data):
    # Dummy save logic
    print(f'Saving data: {data}')

def read_from_database(query):
    # Dummy read logic
    return f'Retrieved data for query: {query}'
```

This separation allows write operations to be optimized and scaled independently from read operations, improving overall system performance.

5. Saga Pattern

The Saga pattern manages distributed transactions across multiple services, ensuring data consistency and handling failures gracefully.

Example:

```python
def saga_step_handler(event, context):
    # Execute transaction step
    try:
        perform_step(event['step'])
```

```
        return {
            'statusCode': 200,
            'body': 'Step completed successfully'
        }
    except Exception as e:
        # Compensate for failure
        compensate_step(event['step'])
        return {
            'statusCode': 500,
            'body': f'Step failed: {str(e)}'
        }

def perform_step(step):
    # Dummy step execution logic
    print(f'Performing step: {step}')

def compensate_step(step):
    # Dummy compensation logic
    print(f'Compensating step: {step}')
```

Serverless functions coordinate the steps of a saga, providing scalability and fault tolerance for distributed transactions.

Traditional architectures often encounter bottlenecks that make scaling painful, such as resource contention, database limitations, and single points of failure.

Serverless architectures, with their inherent scalability and flexibility, provide a robust solution to these challenges. By leveraging scalable software architecture patterns like microservices, event-driven architecture, data lakes, CQRS, and the Saga pattern, developers can design and implement systems that scale efficiently and resiliently.

Serverless systems offer automatic scaling, event-driven execution, and cost-effective resource utilization, making them ideal for modern applications that need to handle variable and unpredictable loads. As you apply these principles and patterns, you'll be able to build scalable, resilient, and efficient applications that can meet the demands of today's digital landscape, ensuring your systems are prepared for growth and change.

The Rise of Serverless: A New Paradigm for Scalable Applications

In the ever-evolving landscape of software development, serverless computing has emerged as a transformative paradigm. By abstracting the underlying infrastructure management and focusing on code execution, serverless architectures have enabled developers to build scalable, efficient, and cost-effective applications. This essay delves into the rise of serverless computing, exploring its core principles, benefits, and how it leverages scalable software architecture patterns to create robust and flexible systems.

The Core Principles of Serverless Computing

Serverless computing, also known as Function-as-a-Service (FaaS), allows developers to run code without provisioning or managing servers. The key principles that underpin serverless computing are:

1. Event-Driven Execution: Serverless functions are triggered by events, such as HTTP requests, database changes, or message queues. This event-driven model allows for asynchronous processing and decoupling of components.

2. Automatic Scaling: Serverless platforms automatically scale functions in response to incoming events. This means that functions can handle any number of concurrent executions, scaling up or down as needed without manual intervention.

3. Pay-Per-Use Pricing: Serverless providers charge based on the number of executions and the duration of each execution, rather than for pre-allocated resources. This model ensures cost efficiency, as users only pay for what they use.

4. Statelessness: Serverless functions are stateless, meaning they do not maintain any internal state between executions. This design promotes horizontal scaling and fault tolerance, as each function execution is independent.

Benefits of Serverless Computing

The adoption of serverless computing brings several significant benefits:

1. Reduced Operational Overhead: By offloading infrastructure management to cloud providers, developers can focus on writing and deploying code. This reduction in operational overhead accelerates development cycles and increases productivity.

2. Scalability: Serverless architectures inherently support horizontal scaling. Functions can automatically scale out to handle increased loads, ensuring that applications remain responsive and performant under varying conditions.

3. Cost Efficiency: The pay-per-use pricing model eliminates the need to over-provision resources. Organizations can achieve cost savings by paying only for the compute time their functions consume, avoiding the costs associated with idle resources.

4. Flexibility and Agility: Serverless functions can be developed, tested, and deployed independently, allowing for greater flexibility and agility. This modular approach enables teams to iterate quickly and adapt to changing requirements.

Leveraging Scalable Software Architecture Patterns in Serverless Systems

Serverless computing excels when combined with scalable software architecture patterns. These patterns provide frameworks for building resilient, maintainable, and scalable applications. Let's explore some key patterns and their implementation in serverless environments.

1. Microservices Architecture

The microservices architecture pattern decomposes applications into smaller, loosely coupled services, each responsible for a specific functionality. In a serverless context, each microservice can be implemented as a set of serverless functions.

Example:

```python
```

```python
# Example of a microservice for user registration
import boto3

dynamodb = boto3.client('dynamodb')

def register_user(event, context):
    # Parse user data from the event
    user_data = event['body']

    # Store user data in DynamoDB
    dynamodb.put_item(
        TableName='Users',
        Item={
            'UserID': {'S': user_data['user_id']},
            'Name': {'S': user_data['name']},
            'Email': {'S': user_data['email']}
        }
    )

    return {
        'statusCode': 200,
        'body': 'User registered successfully'
    }
```

In this example, the `register_user` function handles user registration. Each function in the microservice can scale independently based on its load, ensuring efficient resource utilization.

2. Event-Driven Architecture

Event-driven architecture (EDA) is a natural fit for serverless systems. In EDA, services communicate through events, allowing for asynchronous processing and decoupling of components.

Example:

```python
import boto3

s3 = boto3.client('s3')
sns = boto3.client('sns')

def process_file(event, context):
    # Event triggered by an S3 upload
    bucket = event['Records'][0]['s3']['bucket']['name']
    key = event['Records'][0]['s3']['object']['key']

    # Process the uploaded file
    response = s3.get_object(Bucket=bucket, Key=key)
    content = response['Body'].read().decode('utf-8')

    # Publish a message to SNS after processing
    sns.publish(
```

```
    TopicArn='arn:aws:sns:us-west-
2:123456789012:FileProcessed',
    Message=f'File {key} processed successfully'
)

    return {
        'statusCode': 200,
        'body': 'File processed successfully'
    }
```

Here, an S3 event triggers the `process_file` function, which processes the file and publishes a message to an SNS topic. This decoupled approach allows each component to scale independently.

3. Data Lake Architecture

A data lake architecture stores raw data in its native format, enabling scalable data processing and analytics. Serverless functions can be used to ingest, transform, and analyze data within a data lake.

Example:

```python
import boto3
import json
```

```python
s3 = boto3.client('s3')
glue = boto3.client('glue')

def ingest_data(event, context):
    # Process incoming data and store in S3
    data = event['body']
    s3.put_object(Bucket='data-lake', Key='raw-data/data.json', Body=json.dumps(data))

    # Trigger a Glue job to process the data
    glue.start_job_run(JobName='process-data-job')

    return {
        'statusCode': 200,
        'body': 'Data ingested successfully'
    }
```

In this example, the `ingest_data` function ingests raw data into an S3 bucket, which serves as a data lake. A Glue job processes the data, demonstrating how serverless functions can handle scalable data workflows.

4. CQRS (Command Query Responsibility Segregation)

CQRS separates read and write operations, allowing them to scale independently. In a serverless architecture, separate functions handle commands (writes) and queries (reads).

Example:

```python
# Command (write) function
def create_order(event, context):
    # Create a new order
    order_data = event['body']
    # Store order in the database (e.g., DynamoDB)
    # ...
    return {
       'statusCode': 200,
       'body': 'Order created successfully'
    }

# Query (read) function
def get_order(event, context):
    # Retrieve an order
    order_id = event['pathParameters']['order_id']
    # Fetch order from the database (e.g., DynamoDB)
    # ...
    return {
       'statusCode': 200,
       'body': 'Order details'
```

    }
```

By separating commands and queries, each operation can scale according to its specific load, improving overall system performance.

## 5. Saga Pattern

The Saga pattern manages distributed transactions across multiple services, ensuring data consistency and handling failures gracefully. In serverless architectures, Sagas are implemented as a series of coordinated functions.

**Example**:

```python
def order_saga_step(event, context):
    # Perform a step in the order saga
    step = event['step']

    try:
        perform_step(step)
        return {
            'statusCode': 200,
            'body': 'Step completed successfully'
        }
```
```

```
        except Exception as e:
            # Handle failure and compensation
            compensate_step(step)
            return {
                'statusCode': 500,
                'body': f'Step failed: {str(e)}'
            }

def perform_step(step):
    # Perform the saga step
    # ...

def compensate_step(step):
    # Compensate for the failed step
    # ...
```
```

This example demonstrates a Saga step function that performs a transaction step and compensates for failures, ensuring consistency across distributed services.

The rise of serverless computing marks a significant shift in how applications are developed, deployed, and scaled. By abstracting infrastructure management and focusing on code execution, serverless architectures enable developers to build scalable, efficient, and cost-effective applications. Leveraging scalable software architecture patterns such as microservices, event-driven architecture,
```

data lakes, CQRS, and the Saga pattern, serverless systems can handle the demands of modern workloads with ease.

Serverless computing not only reduces operational overhead but also provides inherent scalability and cost efficiency. Its event-driven nature and stateless design promote flexibility and agility, allowing organizations to innovate rapidly and adapt to changing requirements. As the serverless paradigm continues to evolve, it promises to drive the next generation of scalable, resilient, and maintainable applications, empowering developers to meet the challenges of a dynamic digital landscape.

Chapter 3

Unveiling Serverless Architecture: Core Concepts and Benefits

Serverless Fundamentals: Functions, Events, and APIs

Serverless computing has emerged as a paradigm-shifting model in the realm of cloud computing, offering developers the ability to build and run applications without managing the underlying infrastructure. The serverless model allows for scalable, event-driven architectures that can handle varying loads efficiently. This document explores the fundamentals of serverless computing, focusing on functions, events, and APIs, and provides insights into scalable software architecture patterns for serverless systems.

1. Introduction to Serverless Computing

Serverless computing abstracts the server management, allowing developers to focus on writing code. This approach is facilitated by cloud providers like AWS (Lambda), Azure (Functions), and Google Cloud (Functions), which manage the infrastructure, scaling, and availability of the applications.

2. Functions: The Building Blocks

2.1 What Are Serverless Functions?

Serverless functions, often called Function-as-a-Service (FaaS), are small, stateless pieces of code that execute in response to events. These functions are typically written to perform a single task or a small set of related tasks.

2.2 Writing Serverless Functions

Here's an example of an AWS Lambda function written in Python that processes an image upload:

```python
import boto3
import json

def lambda_handler(event, context):
    s3_client = boto3.client('s3')

    for record in event['Records']:
        bucket = record['s3']['bucket']['name']
        key = record['s3']['object']['key']

        # Perform image processing here

        # Example: Copy the file to another bucket
        copy_source = {'Bucket': bucket, 'Key': key}
```

```
    target_bucket = 'processed-images-bucket'

    s3_client.copy(copy_source, target_bucket, key)

    return {
        'statusCode': 200,
        'body': json.dumps(f'Successfully processed {key}')
    }
```

2.3 Scaling with Serverless Functions

One of the key advantages of serverless functions is their ability to scale automatically. When an event triggers a function, the cloud provider provisions the resources necessary to run the function. If multiple events occur simultaneously, multiple instances of the function can run in parallel, ensuring high availability and performance.

3. Events: Triggers for Serverless Functions

3.1 Event Sources

Events are the triggers that initiate the execution of serverless functions. They can come from various sources, including:

- HTTP requests via API Gateway

- Changes in data (e.g., new records in a database)

- File uploads (e.g., to an S3 bucket)

- Scheduled tasks (e.g., using cron jobs)

- Messaging services (e.g., SNS, SQS)

3.2 Event-Driven Architecture

In an event-driven architecture, functions are designed to respond to events asynchronously. This decoupling of event sources and function logic enhances modularity and scalability. For example, in an e-commerce platform, different functions can handle order placements, payments, and inventory updates, each triggered by respective events.

```json
{
  "Records": [
    {
      "s3": {
        "bucket": {
          "name": "source-bucket"
```

```
    },
    "object": {
      "key": "image.jpg"
  }
```
```

The above JSON structure is an example of an S3 event that triggers a Lambda function when an image is uploaded.

## 4. APIs: Exposing Serverless Functions

### 4.1 API Gateway

API Gateway is a fully managed service that makes it easy for developers to create, publish, maintain, monitor, and secure APIs at any scale. When combined with serverless functions, API Gateway provides a robust platform for building scalable APIs.

### 4.2 Creating a Serverless API

To create a serverless API, you define routes and methods in API Gateway that trigger Lambda functions. Here's an example of a simple serverless API in AWS:

**1. Define the API in API Gateway:**
```

- Create a new API.

- Define resource paths (e.g., `/users`).

- Set up methods (e.g., GET, POST).

2. Connect API Gateway to Lambda:

- Create a Lambda function to handle the API request.

- Configure the method in API Gateway to invoke the Lambda function.

4.3 Example: Serverless REST API

Here's an example of a Lambda function that serves as an endpoint in a REST API:

```python
import json
import boto3

def lambda_handler(event, context):
    dynamodb = boto3.resource('dynamodb')
    table = dynamodb.Table('Users')

    if event['httpMethod'] == 'GET':
```

```
        response = table.scan()
        return {
           'statusCode': 200,
           'body': json.dumps(response['Items'])
        }

    elif event['httpMethod'] == 'POST':
      item = json.loads(event['body'])
      table.put_item(Item=item)
      return {
         'statusCode': 201,
          'body': json.dumps(item)
      }

    return {
       'statusCode': 400,
       'body': json.dumps('Unsupported method')
    }
```

5. Scalable Software Architecture Patterns for Serverless Systems

5.1 Microservices

Serverless architectures naturally align with the microservices pattern, where applications are composed of small, independent services. Each microservice is responsible for a specific business capability and communicates with other services over well-defined APIs.

Benefits of microservices in serverless:

- **Independent scaling:** Each function scales independently based on demand.

- **Fault isolation**: Failures in one service do not affect others.

- **Technology diversity:** Different microservices can use different technologies.

5.2 Event-Driven Patterns

In event-driven architectures, services communicate through events. This pattern is highly scalable and decouples services, allowing them to evolve independently.

- **Event Sourcing**: This pattern involves storing state changes as a sequence of events. For example, instead of storing the final state of an order, store the sequence of events (order placed, order shipped, etc.).

- **CQRS (Command Query Responsibility Segregation):** Separate the models for reading and writing data. Commands modify the state, and queries retrieve the state. This segregation can improve performance and scalability.

5.3 Serverless Messaging Patterns

- **Fan-out Pattern:** Distribute an event to multiple consumers. For instance, an order placed event can trigger functions to update inventory, notify the user, and process payment simultaneously.

- **Choreography Pattern:** Each service performs its task and publishes an event that triggers the next service. This avoids a central orchestrator and allows services to act autonomously.

6. Best Practices for Serverless Architectures

6.1 Function Optimization

- **Minimize Cold Starts:** Keep functions warm using scheduled invocations.

- **Optimize Package Size:** Reduce the size of deployment packages to speed up loading times.

- **Stateless Functions:** Ensure functions are stateless to facilitate scaling and parallelism.

6.2 Monitoring and Logging

- **Centralized Logging:** Use services like AWS CloudWatch or Azure Monitor to aggregate logs.

- **Tracing**: Implement distributed tracing to monitor function execution and performance across services.

6.3 Security

- **Least Privilege Principle:** Grant functions only the permissions they need.

- **Environment Variables:** Use environment variables to manage sensitive information like API keys.

- **Authentication and Authorization:** Use managed services like AWS IAM or Azure AD to handle security.

Serverless computing represents a significant evolution in cloud computing, enabling developers to build scalable, event-driven applications without managing infrastructure. By leveraging functions, events, and APIs, and adhering to scalable software architecture patterns, organizations can achieve high availability, performance, and modularity in their applications. As serverless technology continues to mature, it will undoubtedly become a cornerstone of modern application development.

Event-Driven Communication: Building Loosely Coupled Systems

Event-driven communication is a key architectural pattern for building loosely coupled systems, particularly in the context of serverless computing. This approach enhances the scalability, flexibility, and maintainability of applications by decoupling services and allowing them to communicate asynchronously. In this document, we will explore the fundamentals of event-driven communication, provide examples of its implementation, and discuss scalable software architecture patterns for serverless systems.

Fundamentals of Event-Driven Communication

What is Event-Driven Communication?

Event-driven communication is a design paradigm where services or components interact by emitting and responding to events. An event is a significant change in state or an occurrence within a system, such as a user action, a change in data, or a scheduled task. This paradigm shifts from traditional synchronous communication (e.g., direct API calls) to an asynchronous model where events trigger actions.

Benefits of Event-Driven Communication

1. Decoupling: Services are loosely coupled, reducing dependencies and allowing independent evolution.

2. Scalability: Asynchronous processing and distributed architecture enhance scalability.

3. Resilience: Fault isolation is improved since services operate independently.

4. Flexibility: New services can be added without modifying existing ones.

Core Concepts in Event-Driven Systems

Events and Event Sources

An event is a record of an occurrence within a system. Event sources are entities or services that produce events. Examples include:

- **User actions:** Clicking a button, submitting a form.

- **System operations:** Completing a transaction, updating a record.

- **External triggers:** Receiving an email, a timer elapsing.

Event Consumers

Event consumers are services or components that respond to events. They subscribe to specific events and execute defined actions upon receiving them. Consumers can perform various tasks, such as updating databases, sending notifications, or invoking other services.

Implementing Event-Driven Communication

Example: AWS Serverless Stack

Let's consider an example of an e-commerce application using AWS Lambda, S3, SNS (Simple Notification Service), and DynamoDB to demonstrate event-driven communication.

Step 1: Uploading an Image to S3

When a user uploads an image to an S3 bucket, it triggers an event. Here's the event notification configuration for the S3 bucket:

```json
{
  "Bucket": "source-bucket",
  "NotificationConfiguration": {
    "LambdaFunctionConfigurations": [
      {
        "LambdaFunctionArn": "arn:aws:lambda:us-east-1:123456789012:function:ImageProcessor",
        "Events": ["s3:ObjectCreated:*"]
      }
```

Step 2: Processing the Image with Lambda

The S3 event triggers a Lambda function to process the image:

```python
import boto3
import json

def lambda_handler(event, context):
    s3_client = boto3.client('s3')
    sns_client = boto3.client('sns')
```

```
    for record in event['Records']:
        bucket = record['s3']['bucket']['name']
        key = record['s3']['object']['key']

        # Example image processing task
        processed_key = f'processed/{key}'
        s3_client.copy_object(Bucket=bucket, CopySource={'Bucket': bucket, 'Key': key}, Key=processed_key)

        # Publish event to SNS
        message = {
            'bucket': bucket,
            'key': processed_key
        }
        sns_client.publish(
            TopicArn='arn:aws:sns:us-east-1:123456789012:ImageProcessed',
            Message=json.dumps(message)
        )

    return {
        'statusCode': 200,
        'body': json.dumps('Image processed and event published')
    }
```

Step 3: Consuming the Event with Another Lambda Function

An SNS subscription triggers another Lambda function to update the DynamoDB table:

```python
import boto3
import json

def lambda_handler(event, context):
    dynamodb = boto3.resource('dynamodb')
    table = dynamodb.Table('ProcessedImages')

    sns_message = json.loads(event['Records'][0]['Sns']['Message'])
    bucket = sns_message['bucket']
    key = sns_message['key']

    # Update DynamoDB table
    table.put_item(
      Item={
         'ImageId': key,
         'Bucket': bucket,
         'Status': 'Processed'
      }
    )
```

```
    return {
        'statusCode': 200,
        'body': json.dumps('DynamoDB updated')
    }
```

Scalable Software Architecture Patterns for Event-Driven Systems

Event Sourcing

Event sourcing is a pattern where state changes are stored as a sequence of events. This approach is particularly useful for maintaining an audit trail and reconstructing state. Instead of storing the current state, each state change (event) is logged.

Example: Order Processing System

In an order processing system, instead of directly updating the order status, every change is recorded as an event:

1. Order Placed: Initial event with order details.

2. Payment Processed: Event indicating successful payment.

3. Order Shipped: Event indicating the order has been shipped.

These events can be stored in a database (e.g., DynamoDB, EventStore) and used to reconstruct the order state:

```python
events = [
    {'event_type': 'OrderPlaced', 'order_id': '123', 'details': {...}},
    {'event_type': 'PaymentProcessed', 'order_id': '123', 'details': {...}},
    {'event_type': 'OrderShipped', 'order_id': '123', 'details': {...}}
]

order_state = {}
for event in events:
    if event['event_type'] == 'OrderPlaced':
        order_state = event['details']
    elif event['event_type'] == 'PaymentProcessed':
        order_state['payment_status'] = 'Processed'
    elif event['event_type'] == 'OrderShipped':
        order_state['shipping_status'] = 'Shipped'

print(order_state)
```

```

## Command Query Responsibility Segregation (CQRS)

CQRS separates the write (command) and read (query) operations into different models. This pattern enhances performance, scalability, and security by optimizing the operations independently.

**Example: Inventory Management System**

In an inventory management system, commands (e.g., adding or removing items) are handled by one set of functions, while queries (e.g., checking inventory levels) are handled by another set:

```python
# Command to add inventory
def add_inventory(item_id, quantity):
    dynamodb = boto3.resource('dynamodb')
    table = dynamodb.Table('Inventory')

    table.update_item(
        Key={'ItemId': item_id},
        UpdateExpression='SET Quantity = Quantity + :val',
        ExpressionAttributeValues={':val': quantity}
    )
```
```

```
# Query to get inventory
def get_inventory(item_id):
    dynamodb = boto3.resource('dynamodb')
    table = dynamodb.Table('Inventory')

    response = table.get_item(Key={'ItemId': item_id})
    return response['Item']

# Example usage
add_inventory('item123', 10)
print(get_inventory('item123'))
```
```

## Event-Driven Messaging Patterns

### Fan-out Pattern

The fan-out pattern involves distributing a single event to multiple consumers. This is often achieved using messaging services like SNS, Kafka, or Kinesis. Each consumer performs a different task based on the event.

### Example: Order Placed Event

When an order is placed, multiple services (inventory, billing, shipping) need to act on it:
```

```python
sns_client.publish(
    TopicArn='arn:aws:sns:us-east-1:123456789012:OrderPlaced',
    Message=json.dumps({'order_id': '123', 'details': {...}})
)
```

Each service subscribes to the `OrderPlaced` topic and processes the event independently.

Choreography Pattern

In the choreography pattern, each service performs its task and publishes an event that triggers the next service in the workflow. There is no central orchestrator; services are autonomous.

Example: Order Fulfillment Workflow

1. Order Service: Publishes `OrderPlaced` event.

2. Payment Service: Subscribes to `OrderPlaced`, processes payment, and publishes `PaymentProcessed`.

3. Shipping Service: Subscribes to `PaymentProcessed`, prepares shipment, and publishes `OrderShipped`.

Best Practices for Event-Driven Systems

1. Design for Idempotency

Ensure that event handlers are idempotent, meaning they can handle the same event multiple times without adverse effects. This avoids issues with duplicate event processing.

2. Use Event Versioning

Version your events to handle changes in event structure over time. This allows for backward compatibility and easier evolution of your system.

3. Implement Dead Letter Queues

Use dead letter queues to capture and analyze failed event messages. This helps in troubleshooting and ensuring reliable event processing.

4. Monitor and Log Events

Implement robust monitoring and logging for your event-driven system. Use services like AWS CloudWatch, Azure Monitor, or ELK Stack to track event flows and diagnose issues.

Event-driven communication is a powerful paradigm for building loosely coupled, scalable, and resilient systems. By leveraging serverless technologies and adopting scalable software architecture patterns such as event sourcing, CQRS, and event-driven messaging, organizations can create systems that are not only robust and flexible but also capable of evolving independently. As the adoption of serverless and event-driven architectures grows, understanding and implementing these patterns will become increasingly essential for modern application development.

Advantages of Serverless: Automatic Scaling, Cost Efficiency, and Agility

Serverless computing has revolutionized the way applications are developed and deployed, offering significant advantages over traditional server-based architectures. Among its many benefits, automatic scaling, cost efficiency, and agility stand out as key reasons why organizations are increasingly adopting serverless technologies. This document explores these advantages in detail, supported by examples and scalable software architecture patterns.

1. Automatic Scaling

What is Automatic Scaling?

Automatic scaling, or auto-scaling, refers to the ability of a system to adjust its computational resources dynamically in response to varying workloads. In a serverless environment, this means that the cloud provider automatically provisions and deprovisions resources as needed, ensuring optimal performance without manual intervention.

Benefits of Automatic Scaling

1. Elasticity: Serverless functions can handle sudden spikes in traffic seamlessly, scaling out to meet demand and scaling in when the load decreases.

2. Performance Optimization: Ensures consistent performance by allocating the necessary resources to handle the workload.

3. Operational Simplicity: Developers are relieved from the burden of managing and configuring servers to handle varying loads.

Example: AWS Lambda Automatic Scaling

Consider an online retail application that needs to handle thousands of orders during a flash sale. Using AWS

Lambda, the application can automatically scale to handle the influx of orders:

Step 1: Create a Lambda Function

```python
import boto3
import json

def lambda_handler(event, context):
    dynamodb = boto3.resource('dynamodb')
    table = dynamodb.Table('Orders')

    order = json.loads(event['body'])
    table.put_item(Item=order)

    return {
        'statusCode': 200,
        'body': json.dumps('Order placed successfully')
    }
```

Step 2: Configure API Gateway

Set up an API Gateway to trigger the Lambda function for incoming HTTP requests. API Gateway handles routing, throttling, and security, while Lambda manages the compute scaling.

Step 3: Test Scaling

During peak times, such as flash sales, the Lambda function scales out to handle the high volume of orders, ensuring no user experiences downtime or latency issues.

2. Cost Efficiency

What is Cost Efficiency?

Cost efficiency in a serverless context means that you only pay for the actual compute resources used during the execution of your functions. This pay-as-you-go model eliminates the need for provisioning and paying for idle resources.

Benefits of Cost Efficiency

1. Reduced Overhead: No need to maintain and pay for idle servers or unused capacity.

2. Predictable Billing: Costs are directly related to usage, making it easier to predict and control expenses.

3. Optimized Resource Utilization: Only the exact amount of compute power required is allocated, minimizing waste.

Example: AWS Lambda Cost Efficiency

Step 1: Define a Lambda Function for a Real-time Data Processing Task

```python
import boto3
import json

def lambda_handler(event, context):
    s3_client = boto3.client('s3')
    s3_bucket = 'data-bucket'

    for record in event['Records']:
        key = record['s3']['object']['key']

        # Process the data file
        response = s3_client.get_object(Bucket=s3_bucket, Key=key)
        data = response['Body'].read().decode('utf-8')

        # Perform data processing (e.g., parse CSV, update database, etc.)

    return {
        'statusCode': 200,
        'body': json.dumps('Data processed successfully')
```

    }
...

Step 2: Trigger Lambda with S3 Event Notifications

Configure an S3 bucket to trigger the Lambda function whenever a new data file is uploaded. This ensures that the function only runs when there is work to be done, optimizing costs.

Step 3: Analyze Cost Efficiency

By using Lambda, you only pay for the time the function runs and the number of executions, eliminating the need to provision and pay for a constantly running server.

3. Agility

What is Agility?

Agility in software development refers to the ability to rapidly develop, test, and deploy applications. Serverless architectures enhance agility by abstracting infrastructure management, allowing developers to focus on writing and deploying code.

Benefits of Agility

1. Faster Development Cycles: Developers can quickly deploy and update functions without dealing with infrastructure.

2. Ease of Experimentation: Serverless platforms facilitate rapid prototyping and testing of new ideas.

3. Simplified Operations: Infrastructure concerns are offloaded to the cloud provider, allowing teams to concentrate on core application logic.

Example: Agile Development with AWS Lambda and API Gateway

Step 1: Develop a Lambda Function for a New Feature

```python
import json

def lambda_handler(event, context):
    message = json.loads(event['body'])['message']

    # Perform some business logic with the message
    processed_message = f"Processed: {message}"

    return {
        'statusCode': 200,
```

```
    'body': json.dumps({'message':
processed_message})
    }
```

Step 2: Deploy and Integrate with API Gateway

Deploy the function and integrate it with API Gateway to expose it as a REST API. This can be done using tools like AWS SAM (Serverless Application Model) or the AWS Management Console.

Step 3: Iterate and Deploy Updates

As new requirements emerge or bugs are discovered, updates to the Lambda function can be deployed quickly, without downtime. The deployment process is streamlined, supporting continuous integration and continuous delivery (CI/CD) practices.

Scalable Software Architecture Patterns for Serverless Systems

1. Microservices

Serverless architectures align well with the microservices pattern, where applications are composed of small, independent services. Each service performs a specific business function and communicates over well-defined APIs.

Example: E-commerce Platform

An e-commerce platform can be broken down into various microservices such as user management, order processing, inventory management, and payment processing. Each microservice is implemented as a set of serverless functions that handle specific tasks:

```python
# User Management Service
def create_user(event, context):
    # Code to create a user
    pass

def get_user(event, context):
    # Code to retrieve user details
    pass

# Order Processing Service
def create_order(event, context):
    # Code to create an order
    pass

def get_order(event, context):
    # Code to retrieve order details
```

```
    pass

# Deploy each function independently and use API Gateway for communication.
```

2. Event-Driven Architecture

Event-driven architecture (EDA) is a pattern where services communicate through events. This enhances decoupling and allows services to react to state changes asynchronously.

Example: Order Fulfillment

1. Order Service: Publishes an `OrderPlaced` event when a new order is created.

2. Inventory Service: Subscribes to `OrderPlaced` events to update stock levels.

3. Shipping Service: Subscribes to `OrderPlaced` events to initiate shipping.

```python
# Order Service
import boto3
```

```python
def create_order(event, context):
    # Code to create an order
    sns_client = boto3.client('sns')
    sns_client.publish(
        TopicArn='arn:aws:sns:us-east-1:123456789012:OrderPlaced',
        Message=json.dumps({'order_id': '123', 'details': {...}})
    )

# Inventory Service
def update_inventory(event, context):
    sns_message = json.loads(event['Records'][0]['Sns']['Message'])
    order_id = sns_message['order_id']
    # Code to update inventory based on the order
    pass

# Shipping Service
def initiate_shipping(event, context):
    sns_message = json.loads(event['Records'][0]['Sns']['Message'])
    order_id = sns_message['order_id']
    # Code to initiate shipping based on the order
    pass
```

Serverless computing offers compelling advantages, including automatic scaling, cost efficiency, and agility. By leveraging serverless platforms like AWS Lambda, Azure Functions, and Google Cloud Functions, developers can build scalable, cost-effective, and flexible applications. Adopting scalable software architecture patterns such as microservices and event-driven architectures further enhances these benefits, enabling organizations to create robust and maintainable systems. As serverless technology continues to evolve, its adoption will likely grow, driving innovation and efficiency in software development.

Chapter 4

Stateless Function Principles: Avoiding State Management for Scalability

Stateless functions, a fundamental principle in serverless computing, offer numerous advantages for building scalable and efficient applications. By eliminating the need for state management within functions, developers can create systems that are highly scalable, resilient, and easy to maintain. In this document, we will explore the principles of stateless functions, their benefits, and how they contribute to scalable software architecture patterns in serverless systems.

Understanding Stateless Functions

What are Stateless Functions?

Stateless functions, also known as "pure" functions, are functions that do not maintain any state or memory between invocations. They operate solely on their inputs, producing deterministic outputs based on those inputs. In the context of serverless computing, stateless functions are the building blocks of applications, each performing a specific task or handling a particular event.

Benefits of Stateless Functions

1. Scalability: Stateless functions are inherently scalable, as they can be invoked independently and in parallel without concerns about shared state or resource contention.

2. Fault Tolerance: Since stateless functions do not rely on external state, failures in one function instance do not affect others, ensuring fault isolation and resilience.

3. Simplicity: Stateless functions are easier to reason about and debug, as their behavior is solely determined by their inputs and not influenced by external factors.

Principles of Stateless Function Design

1. No External State Dependency

Stateless functions should not rely on external state, such as database connections, file systems, or shared memory. Instead, they should receive all necessary inputs as parameters and return outputs based solely on those inputs.

2. Idempotence

Stateless functions should be idempotent, meaning that invoking the function multiple times with the same inputs should produce the same result. This property ensures predictable behavior and fault tolerance.

3. No Side Effects

Stateless functions should not produce any side effects, such as modifying external state or interacting with external resources. They should only compute outputs based on inputs and avoid any actions that could introduce hidden dependencies or alter the system's state.

4. Horizontal Scalability

Stateless functions should be designed for horizontal scalability, allowing them to scale out by adding more function instances to handle increasing workloads. This scalability pattern enables efficient resource utilization and high throughput.

Implementing Stateless Functions in Serverless Architectures

Example: AWS Lambda Function

```python
import json

def lambda_handler(event, context):
```

```
    # Process input event
    input_data = json.loads(event['body'])

    # Perform computation
    result = perform_computation(input_data)

    # Return result
    return {
       'statusCode': 200,
       'body': json.dumps(result)
    }

def perform_computation(input_data):
    # Stateless computation logic
    return input_data * 2
```

In the above example, the `lambda_handler` function is stateless and receives input data as an event parameter. It performs a computation based on the input data and returns the result. The function does not rely on external state or produce any side effects, adhering to the principles of stateless function design.

Stateless Functions and Scalable Software Architecture Patterns

Microservices

Stateless functions align well with the microservices architecture pattern, where applications are composed of small, independent services that communicate via APIs. Each microservice can be implemented as a set of stateless functions, performing specific business functions or handling individual tasks.

Example: E-commerce Platform

An e-commerce platform can be decomposed into microservices such as user management, product catalog, order processing, and payment processing. Each microservice can be implemented as a set of stateless functions, allowing for independent scaling, deployment, and maintenance.

```python
# User Management Microservice
def create_user(event, context):
    # Stateless function to create a new user
    pass

def get_user(event, context):
    # Stateless function to retrieve user details
    pass

# Product Catalog Microservice
```

```python
def list_products(event, context):
    # Stateless function to list available products
    pass

def get_product(event, context):
    # Stateless function to retrieve product details
    pass

# Order Processing Microservice
def create_order(event, context):
    # Stateless function to create a new order
    pass

def get_order(event, context):
    # Stateless function to retrieve order details
    pass

# Payment Processing Microservice
def process_payment(event, context):
    # Stateless function to process payment for an order
    pass
```
```

Each function within the microservices is stateless and operates independently, allowing for horizontal scaling and fault isolation.

### Event-Driven Architecture
```

Stateless functions are a key component of event-driven architectures, where services communicate asynchronously via events. In event-driven systems, functions react to events by performing specific actions or computations, without relying on shared state or coordination.

Example: Order Fulfillment Workflow

1. Order Service: Receives an order event and creates a new order.

2. Inventory Service: Subscribes to order events and updates inventory levels.

3. Shipping Service: Subscribes to order events and initiates shipping for new orders.

```python
# Order Service
def create_order(event, context):
    # Stateless function to create a new order
    pass

# Inventory Service
def update_inventory(event, context):
```

```
    # Stateless function to update inventory levels based on order events
    pass

# Shipping Service
def initiate_shipping(event, context):
    # Stateless function to initiate shipping for new orders
    pass
```

Each function in the workflow is stateless and reacts to order events independently, ensuring scalability, fault tolerance, and loose coupling.

Stateless functions are a fundamental principle in serverless computing, offering numerous benefits for building scalable, resilient, and efficient applications. By adhering to the principles of stateless function design and leveraging stateless functions in scalable software architecture patterns such as microservices and event-driven architectures, organizations can create systems that are highly adaptable, fault-tolerant, and easy to maintain. As serverless technology continues to evolve, the importance of stateless functions in enabling scalable and efficient computing paradigms will only increase, driving innovation and agility in modern application development.

Decomposing Workflows into Smaller, Independent Functions

Decomposing workflows into smaller, independent functions is a foundational principle in serverless computing. By breaking down complex processes into discrete tasks, developers can create scalable, maintainable, and agile applications. In this document, we will explore the benefits of decomposing workflows, discuss strategies for breaking down workflows into functions, and provide examples of how this approach aligns with scalable software architecture patterns for serverless systems.

Understanding Workflow Decomposition

What is Workflow Decomposition?

Workflow decomposition involves breaking down a larger business process or task into smaller, more manageable units of work. Each unit, or function, is responsible for performing a specific task or handling a particular aspect of the workflow. By decomposing workflows into functions, developers can achieve greater flexibility, scalability, and modularity in their applications.

Benefits of Workflow Decomposition

1. Scalability: Smaller functions can be independently scaled to meet varying workloads, ensuring optimal resource utilization and performance.

2. Modularity: Decomposed workflows promote code reuse and maintainability, as individual functions can be developed, tested, and deployed independently.

3. Agility: Breaking down workflows into smaller units enables rapid iteration and experimentation, fostering a culture of innovation and responsiveness.

Strategies for Decomposing Workflows

1. Identify Independent Tasks

Analyze the workflow to identify tasks or steps that can be performed independently of each other. These tasks can often be implemented as separate functions, allowing for parallel execution and scalability.

2. Define Input and Output Interfaces

Establish clear input and output interfaces for each function, specifying the data format and communication protocols. This ensures interoperability and enables functions to communicate seamlessly within the workflow.

3. Minimize Dependencies

Reduce dependencies between functions by designing them to be as independent as possible. Minimizing dependencies simplifies deployment, improves fault tolerance, and enhances flexibility.

4. Leverage Event-Driven Architecture

Utilize event-driven architecture to coordinate the execution of functions and orchestrate the workflow. Events can trigger functions, propagate data between them, and coordinate their execution in response to changes or events within the system.

Implementing Workflow Decomposition with Serverless Functions

Example: E-commerce Order Processing Workflow

Consider an e-commerce platform's order processing workflow, which involves multiple steps such as order validation, inventory management, payment processing, and shipping. Each step can be implemented as a separate serverless function, facilitating scalability, modularity, and agility.

1. Order Validation Function

```python
import json

def validate_order(event, context):
    order_data = json.loads(event['body'])

    # Perform order validation logic
    if order_data['total_amount'] > 0:
        return {
            'statusCode': 200,
            'body': json.dumps({'message': 'Order validated successfully'})
        }
    else:
        return {
            'statusCode': 400,
            'body': json.dumps({'message': 'Invalid order'})
        }
```

2. Inventory Management Function

```python
```

```python
import json

def update_inventory(event, context):
    order_data = json.loads(event['body'])
    product_id = order_data['product_id']
    quantity = order_data['quantity']

    # Update inventory levels
    # Code to update inventory
```

3. Payment Processing Function

```python
import json

def process_payment(event, context):
    order_data = json.loads(event['body'])
    payment_amount = order_data['total_amount']

    # Process payment
    # Code to process payment
```

4. Shipping Function

```python
import json
```

```
def initiate_shipping(event, context):
    order_data = json.loads(event['body'])
    shipping_address = order_data['shipping_address']

    # Initiate shipping
    # Code to initiate shipping
```
```

## Scalable Software Architecture Patterns for Decomposed Workflows

### Microservices

Decomposing workflows into smaller, independent functions aligns well with the microservices architecture pattern. Each function can be implemented as a microservice, responsible for a specific task or business capability. Microservices communicate via APIs, enabling loose coupling and independent deployment.

**Example: E-commerce Microservices**

- **Order Service:** Validates orders and manages order lifecycle.

- **Inventory Service:** Handles inventory updates and stock management.
```

- **Payment Service:** Processes payments and manages payment transactions.

- **Shipping Service:** Manages shipping logistics and fulfillment.

Event-Driven Architecture

Event-driven architecture is a natural fit for orchestrating decomposed workflows, allowing functions to react to events and coordinate their execution dynamically. Events can trigger functions, propagate data between them, and coordinate their interaction based on changes or events within the system.

Example: Order Processing Workflow

1. Order Placed Event: Triggers the order validation function.

2. Order Validated Event: Triggers the inventory management and payment processing functions.

3. Inventory Updated Event: Triggers the shipping function to initiate shipping.

Best Practices for Decomposing Workflows

1. Keep Functions Small and Focused: Each function should perform a single task or handle a specific aspect of the workflow, promoting modularity and maintainability.

2. Design for Idempotence: Functions should be idempotent, ensuring that executing them multiple times produces the same result.

3. Handle Errors Gracefully: Implement error handling and retries to ensure fault tolerance and reliability.

4. Use Asynchronous Communication: Utilize asynchronous communication patterns such as messaging queues or event streams to facilitate loose coupling and resilience.

5. Monitor and Measure Performance: Implement monitoring and logging to track the performance and behavior of functions, enabling optimization and troubleshooting.

6. Automate Deployment and Scaling: Leverage automation tools and infrastructure-as-code practices to streamline deployment and scaling of functions, reducing operational overhead and complexity.

Decomposing workflows into smaller, independent functions is a key strategy for building scalable, resilient, and maintainable serverless systems. By breaking down complex processes into discrete tasks and implementing them as serverless functions, developers can achieve greater flexibility, modularity, and agility in their applications. Leveraging scalable software architecture patterns such as microservices and event-driven architecture further enhances the benefits of workflow decomposition, enabling efficient resource utilization, fault tolerance, and responsiveness. As organizations continue to adopt serverless computing, mastering the art of decomposing workflows into functions will be essential for driving innovation and delivering value in today's fast-paced digital landscape.

Handling Long-Running Processes: Asynchronous Workflows and Queues

Handling long-running processes efficiently is crucial for building scalable and responsive applications. In serverless systems, asynchronous workflows and message queues play a vital role in managing tasks that require extended processing times. In this document, we will explore the principles of handling long-running processes, discuss strategies for implementing asynchronous workflows and queues, and provide examples with codes based on scalable software architecture patterns for serverless systems.

Understanding Long-Running Processes

What are Long-Running Processes?

Long-running processes are tasks or workflows that require significant time to complete, often due to factors such as large data volumes, complex computations, or external dependencies. Examples include batch processing, data analytics, image/video processing, and background tasks like email notifications or report generation.

Challenges of Long-Running Processes

1. Blocking Execution: Long-running processes can block the execution of other tasks, leading to reduced system responsiveness and scalability.

2. Resource Consumption: Prolonged execution times may tie up resources, impacting the overall performance and efficiency of the system.

3. Fault Tolerance: Ensuring fault tolerance and resilience becomes challenging when dealing with tasks that span extended periods.

Strategies for Handling Long-Running Processes

1. Asynchronous Workflows

Asynchronous workflows decouple the initiation and completion of tasks, allowing the system to continue processing other requests while long-running tasks execute in the background. This approach enhances system responsiveness and scalability.

2. Message Queues

Message queues provide a mechanism for distributing tasks or messages across multiple consumers asynchronously. Tasks are placed onto a queue and processed by consumers in a scalable and fault-tolerant manner, ensuring efficient resource utilization and fault isolation.

Implementing Asynchronous Workflows and Queues in Serverless Systems

Example: Image Processing Workflow

Consider an image processing application where users upload images for resizing and compression. The image processing task may take significant time, especially for large images. Let's implement this workflow using an asynchronous approach with AWS Lambda and Amazon Simple Queue Service (SQS).

Step 1: Upload Image Handler

```python
import json
import boto3

sqs = boto3.client('sqs')
queue_url = 'your_sqs_queue_url'

def lambda_handler(event, context):
    # Extract image data from the event
    image_data = json.loads(event['body'])

    # Place image processing task onto SQS queue
    response = sqs.send_message(
        QueueUrl=queue_url,
        MessageBody=json.dumps(image_data)
    )

    return {
        'statusCode': 200,
        'body': json.dumps('Image processing task queued successfully')
    }
```

Step 2: Image Processing Worker

```python
import json
import boto3

s3 = boto3.client('s3')
queue_url = 'your_sqs_queue_url'

def lambda_handler(event, context):
    # Retrieve image processing task from SQS
    messages = sqs.receive_message(
        QueueUrl=queue_url,
        MaxNumberOfMessages=1
    )

    if 'Messages' in messages:
        message = messages['Messages'][0]
        image_data = json.loads(message['Body'])

        # Perform image processing (resize, compress, etc.)
        # Code to process the image

        # Delete message from the queue
        receipt_handle = message['ReceiptHandle']
        sqs.delete_message(
            QueueUrl=queue_url,
```

```
        ReceiptHandle=receipt_handle
    )

    return {
        'statusCode': 200,
        'body': json.dumps('Image processed successfully')
    }
```

Scalable Software Architecture Patterns for Long-Running Processes

1. Microservices

Implementing long-running processes as microservices allows for independent scalability, fault tolerance, and maintainability. Each microservice can handle a specific aspect of the workflow, such as image processing, data analysis, or background tasks, and communicate asynchronously with other services via message queues or events.

Example: Microservices for Image Processing

- **Image Processing Service:** Responsible for processing images, resizing, compressing, and applying filters.

- **Notification Service:** Sends notifications to users when image processing is complete.

- **Analytics Service:** Collects and analyzes data on image processing performance and usage patterns.

2. Event-Driven Architecture

Utilizing event-driven architecture enables seamless integration and coordination of long-running processes within the system. Events can trigger the initiation of tasks, propagate data between services, and signal completion or failure, allowing for dynamic and responsive workflows.

Example: Event-Driven Image Processing Workflow

1. Image Uploaded Event: Triggers the initiation of the image processing task.

2. Image Processed Event: Signals the completion of image processing, enabling subsequent actions such as notifications or data updates.

Best Practices for Handling Long-Running Processes

1. Use Idempotent Operations: Ensure that long-running tasks are idempotent, meaning they produce the same result regardless of how many times they are executed. This ensures reliability and fault tolerance.

2. Implement Retry Logic: Implement retry logic for handling transient failures and intermittent errors, ensuring robustness and resilience in long-running processes.

3. Monitor and Track Progress: Implement monitoring and tracking mechanisms to monitor the progress and status of long-running processes, enabling visibility and troubleshooting.

4. Set Timeouts and Limits: Set appropriate timeouts and limits for long-running processes to prevent resource exhaustion and ensure timely completion.

5. Scale Dynamically: Design the system to scale dynamically based on workload and demand, leveraging auto-scaling capabilities to allocate resources as needed.

Handling long-running processes efficiently is essential for building scalable, responsive, and resilient serverless systems. By leveraging asynchronous workflows and message queues, developers can decouple tasks, distribute workloads, and ensure efficient resource utilization. Implementing scalable software architecture patterns such as microservices and event-driven architecture further enhances the benefits of handling long-running processes, enabling agility, fault tolerance, and scalability. As organizations continue to adopt serverless computing, mastering the art of handling long-running processes will be essential for delivering high-performance and reliable applications in today's dynamic and demanding environments.

Chapter 5

Event-Driven Scalability: Orchestrating Services with Asynchronous Messaging

The Power of Events: Reacting to Changes in Real-Time

In modern software architectures, achieving scalability and resilience is a critical requirement, especially for serverless systems. Event-driven scalability, facilitated by asynchronous messaging, offers a powerful approach to building systems that can efficiently handle varying loads and react to changes in real-time. This document explores the principles of event-driven scalability, the benefits of orchestrating services with asynchronous messaging, and provides practical examples with code to illustrate these concepts within the context of scalable software architecture patterns for serverless systems.

Understanding Event-Driven Scalability

What is Event-Driven Scalability?

Event-driven scalability refers to the ability of a system to dynamically scale its components in response to events. In an event-driven architecture, services communicate through events, which are messages indicating a change in state or the occurrence of an action. This approach allows systems to react to events asynchronously, decoupling service interactions and enabling independent scaling of individual components.

Benefits of Event-Driven Scalability

1. Decoupling: Services are loosely coupled, communicating via events rather than direct calls, enhancing modularity and maintainability.

2. Scalability: Services can scale independently based on the volume of events they need to process, improving resource utilization and performance.

3. Resilience: Failures in one service do not directly impact others, as event-driven architectures inherently support fault isolation and recovery.

4. Real-Time Reactions: Systems can react to changes in real-time, enabling immediate processing and responses to events.

Principles of Asynchronous Messaging

Asynchronous Messaging Basics

Asynchronous messaging involves the use of message queues or event streams to facilitate communication between services. Messages are sent to a queue or stream and processed by consumers independently, allowing for asynchronous and parallel processing.

Key Components

1. Producers: Services that generate and publish events or messages.

2. Consumers: Services that receive and process events or messages.

3. Message Broker: The intermediary that manages the message queues or event streams, ensuring reliable delivery and handling of messages.

Implementing Event-Driven Scalability with Serverless Systems

Example: Real-Time Order Processing System

Consider an e-commerce platform where orders are placed by customers, and the system needs to process these orders in real-time. The processing involves multiple steps such as inventory checking, payment processing, and shipping initiation. Implementing this with an event-driven approach ensures scalability and real-time reactions.

Step 1: Order Placement Service

```python
import json
import boto3

sqs = boto3.client('sqs')
order_queue_url = 'your_order_queue_url'

def lambda_handler(event, context):
    order_data = json.loads(event['body'])

    # Publish order event to SQS queue
    sqs.send_message(
        QueueUrl=order_queue_url,
        MessageBody=json.dumps(order_data)
    )

    return {
        'statusCode': 200,
        'body': json.dumps('Order placed successfully')
    }
```

Step 2: Inventory Checking Service

```python
```

```python
import json
import boto3

sqs = boto3.client('sqs')
inventory_queue_url = 'your_inventory_queue_url'

def lambda_handler(event, context):
    # Receive order event from SQS
    for record in event['Records']:
        order_data = json.loads(record['body'])

        # Perform inventory check
        if check_inventory(order_data['product_id'], order_data['quantity']):
            # Publish inventory checked event to SQS
            sqs.send_message(
                QueueUrl=inventory_queue_url,
                MessageBody=json.dumps(order_data)
            )
        else:
            # Handle out-of-stock scenario
            handle_out_of_stock(order_data)

def check_inventory(product_id, quantity):
    # Check inventory logic
    return True

def handle_out_of_stock(order_data):
```

        # Out-of-stock handling logic
        pass
```

### Step 3: Payment Processing Service

```python
import json
import boto3

sqs = boto3.client('sqs')
shipping_queue_url = 'your_shipping_queue_url'

def lambda_handler(event, context):
    # Receive inventory checked event from SQS
    for record in event['Records']:
        order_data = json.loads(record['body'])

        # Process payment
        if process_payment(order_data['payment_details']):
            # Publish payment processed event to SQS
            sqs.send_message(
                QueueUrl=shipping_queue_url,
                MessageBody=json.dumps(order_data)
            )
        else:
            # Handle payment failure
            handle_payment_failure(order_data)

```python
def process_payment(payment_details):
    # Payment processing logic
    return True

def handle_payment_failure(order_data):
    # Payment failure handling logic
    pass
```

Step 4: Shipping Initiation Service

```python
import json

def lambda_handler(event, context):
    # Receive payment processed event from SQS
    for record in event['Records']:
        order_data = json.loads(record['body'])

        # Initiate shipping
        initiate_shipping(order_data)

def initiate_shipping(order_data):
    # Shipping initiation logic
    pass
```

Scalable Software Architecture Patterns for Event-Driven System

Microservices

Event-driven scalability fits naturally with the microservices architecture pattern. Each service in a microservices architecture can operate independently and scale based on the volume of events it processes. This modular approach enhances maintainability and enables independent deployment and scaling.

Example: Microservices for Order Processing

- **Order Service:** Handles order placements and publishes order events.

- **Inventory Service:** Checks inventory and publishes inventory checked events.

- **Payment Service:** Processes payments and publishes payment processed events.

- **Shipping Service:** Initiates shipping based on payment processed events.

Event-Driven Architecture

Event-driven architecture ensures that services communicate and coordinate through events. This approach decouples services, enabling independent scaling and real-time reactions to changes.

Example: Event-Driven Order Processing Workflow

1. Order Placed Event: Triggers inventory checking.

2. Inventory Checked Event: Triggers payment processing.

3. Payment Processed Event: Triggers shipping initiation.

Best Practices for Implementing Event-Driven Scalability

1. Design for Idempotence: Ensure that event handlers are idempotent, meaning processing the same event multiple times does not change the outcome.

2. Implement Robust Error Handling: Handle errors gracefully and implement retries to ensure reliability.

3. Use Dead-Letter Queues: Configure dead-letter queues to capture events that cannot be processed after multiple attempts, enabling troubleshooting and error resolution.

4. Monitor and Optimize: Continuously monitor the performance of event-driven workflows and optimize for efficiency and scalability.

5. Ensure Event Ordering: When necessary, ensure that events are processed in the correct order to maintain data consistency and integrity.

Event-driven scalability, enabled by asynchronous messaging, provides a robust and efficient approach to building scalable and resilient serverless systems. By orchestrating services through events, developers can achieve loose coupling, independent scaling, and real-time responsiveness. Leveraging scalable software architecture patterns such as microservices and event-driven architecture further enhances the benefits of this approach, enabling systems to handle varying loads and react to changes dynamically. As organizations increasingly adopt serverless computing, mastering event-driven scalability will be essential for delivering high-performance, scalable, and resilient applications in today's fast-paced digital environment.

Designing Scalable Event Pipelines: Producers, Consumers, and Error Handling

In modern serverless architectures, designing scalable event pipelines is crucial for ensuring efficient and reliable data processing. Event pipelines allow systems to handle high volumes of data and events in a decoupled and scalable manner. This document explores the principles of designing scalable event pipelines, focusing on producers, consumers, and error handling. We'll delve into scalable software architecture patterns, provide practical examples with code, and discuss best practices for implementing robust event pipelines in serverless systems.

Understanding Event Pipelines

What is an Event Pipeline?

An event pipeline is a sequence of processes where events are generated, transmitted, processed, and stored. The pipeline typically consists of three main components:

- **Producers**: Services that generate and publish events.

- **Consumers**: Services that receive and process events.

- **Message Broker:** The intermediary that transports events from producers to consumers, ensuring reliable delivery and managing event flow.

Benefits of Event Pipelines

1. Scalability: Each component of the pipeline can scale independently to handle varying loads.

2. Decoupling: Producers and consumers are loosely coupled, enabling flexibility and independent development.

3. Resilience: The system can handle failures gracefully, as events can be retried or rerouted.

4. Real-Time Processing: Events can be processed in real-time, enabling immediate reactions to changes.

Designing Producers

Characteristics of Effective Producers

Producers are responsible for generating events and publishing them to the message broker. Effective producers should be:

- **Reliable**: Ensure that events are published successfully.

- **Efficient**: Minimize latency and overhead in event generation.

- **Scalable**: Handle high volumes of events without degradation in performance.

Example: Order Placement Producer

Consider an e-commerce platform where placing an order generates an event. We'll use AWS Lambda and Amazon Simple Queue Service (SQS) to implement the producer.

Order Placement Producer Code

```python
import json
import boto3

sqs = boto3.client('sqs')
order_queue_url = 'your_order_queue_url'
```

```
def lambda_handler(event, context):
    order_data = json.loads(event['body'])

    # Publish order event to SQS queue
    response = sqs.send_message(
        QueueUrl=order_queue_url,
        MessageBody=json.dumps(order_data)
    )

    return {
        'statusCode': 200,
        'body': json.dumps('Order placed successfully')
    }
```

Designing Consumers

Characteristics of Effective Consumers

Consumers are responsible for receiving and processing events. Effective consumers should be:

- **Idempotent**: Ensure that processing the same event multiple times does not affect the outcome.

- **Efficient**: Process events quickly and with minimal resource usage.

- **Scalable**: Handle increasing volumes of events by scaling horizontally.

Example: Order Processing Consumer

Continuing with our e-commerce example, we'll implement an order processing consumer using AWS Lambda and SQS.

Order Processing Consumer Code

```python
import json
import boto3

def lambda_handler(event, context):
    # Receive order events from SQS
    for record in event['Records']:
        order_data = json.loads(record['body'])

        # Process the order
        process_order(order_data)

    return {
        'statusCode': 200,
        'body': json.dumps('Orders processed successfully')
    }
```

```
def process_order(order_data):
    # Order processing logic
    print(f"Processing order: {order_data['order_id']}")
```

Implementing Error Handling

Robust error handling is essential for maintaining the reliability and resilience of event pipelines. Proper error handling ensures that:

- **Failures are detected and managed:** Preventing data loss and ensuring processing continuity.

- **Retries are implemented:** Handling transient errors without manual intervention.

- **Dead-letter queues are used:** Capturing and analyzing failed events for troubleshooting.

Strategies for Error Handling

1. Retries: Implement automatic retries for transient failures, using exponential backoff strategies to avoid overwhelming the system.

2. Dead-Letter Queues (DLQs): Configure DLQs to capture events that fail to process after multiple attempts, enabling analysis and resolution.

3. Monitoring and Alerts: Set up monitoring and alerting mechanisms to detect and respond to failures promptly.

Example: Enhanced Order Processing with Error Handling

We'll enhance our order processing consumer to include retries and DLQ handling.

Enhanced Order Processing Consumer Code

```python
import json
import boto3
import logging
import time

logger = logging.getLogger()
logger.setLevel(logging.INFO)

sqs = boto3.client('sqs')
dlq_url = 'your_dead_letter_queue_url'
```

```python
def lambda_handler(event, context):
    for record in event['Records']:
        order_data = json.loads(record['body'])

        try:
            # Process the order
            process_order(order_data)
        except Exception as e:
            logger.error(f"Error processing order {order_data['order_id']}: {e}")
            handle_failure(record)

    return {
        'statusCode': 200,
        'body': json.dumps('Orders processed successfully')
    }

def process_order(order_data):
    # Simulate random failures
    if order_data['order_id'] % 2 == 0:
        raise Exception("Simulated processing failure")

    logger.info(f"Processing order: {order_data['order_id']}")

def handle_failure(record):
    # Implement retry logic
```

```
retries = record.get('attributes',
{}).get('ApproximateReceiveCount', 1)

if retries > 3:
    # Send to DLQ after 3 retries
    sqs.send_message(
        QueueUrl=dlq_url,
        MessageBody=record['body']
    )
else:
    # Delay and retry
    time.sleep(2 ** retries)
    raise Exception("Retrying")
```

Scalable Software Architecture Patterns

Microservices

Microservices architecture is well-suited for event pipelines, allowing independent scaling and deployment of producers and consumers. Each microservice handles a specific domain, communicating through events and message brokers.

Example: Microservices for E-Commerce

- **Order Service:** Generates order events.

- **Inventory Service:** Processes inventory-related events.

- **Payment Service:** Handles payment processing events.

- **Shipping Service:** Manages shipping-related events.

Event-Driven Architecture

Event-driven architecture decouples services, enabling them to react to events asynchronously. This pattern enhances scalability and fault tolerance.

Example: Event-Driven E-Commerce Workflow

1. Order Placed Event: Triggers inventory checking.

2. Inventory Checked Event: Triggers payment processing.

3. Payment Processed Event: Triggers shipping initiation.

Best Practices for Designing Event Pipelines

1. Design for Idempotence: Ensure that consumers can handle duplicate events without adverse effects.

2. Implement Monitoring and Logging: Use monitoring tools to track event processing and detect issues.

3. Use Exponential Backoff for Retries: Implement exponential backoff strategies to handle transient errors.

4. Leverage Dead-Letter Queues: Configure DLQs to capture and analyze failed events.

5. Ensure Security and Compliance: Secure event data and comply with relevant regulations and standards.

Designing scalable event pipelines is a fundamental aspect of building robust and efficient serverless systems. By leveraging producers, consumers, and asynchronous messaging, developers can create decoupled, scalable, and resilient architectures. Implementing robust error handling mechanisms, such as retries and dead-letter queues, further enhances the reliability of event pipelines. Adopting scalable software architecture patterns like microservices and event-driven architecture enables systems to handle high volumes of data and react to changes in real-time. As organizations continue to embrace serverless computing, mastering the design of scalable event pipelines will be essential for delivering high-performance and reliable applications in today's dynamic digital landscape.

Implementing Fan-Out and Fan-In Patterns for Increased Throughput

In modern serverless architectures, achieving high throughput and scalability is essential for processing large volumes of data efficiently. The fan-out and fan-in patterns are powerful techniques used to distribute workloads across multiple parallel processes and then aggregate the results. This document explores the principles of these patterns, their benefits, and provides practical examples with code to illustrate their implementation in scalable serverless systems.

Understanding Fan-Out and Fan-In Patterns

What is Fan-Out?

Fan-out refers to the process of distributing a single task into multiple smaller tasks that can be processed in parallel. This pattern is useful when dealing with large datasets or computationally intensive tasks, as it allows for concurrent processing, reducing overall processing time.

What is Fan-In?

Fan-in is the complementary process of aggregating results from multiple parallel tasks back into a single output. This pattern ensures that the results of distributed tasks are collected and combined, providing a unified result for the original task.

Benefits of Fan-Out and Fan-In Patterns

1. Increased Throughput: By distributing tasks, the system can handle higher volumes of data and requests simultaneously.
2. Reduced Latency: Parallel processing of tasks reduces the time required to complete complex or large-scale operations.
3. Scalability: The patterns allow the system to scale horizontally by adding more processing units as needed.
4. Fault Tolerance: Failures in individual tasks can be isolated and retried without affecting the overall system performance.

Implementing Fan-Out and Fan-In in Serverless Systems

Example: Image Processing Pipeline

Consider an image processing application where users upload images to be resized and filtered. The fan-out pattern will distribute each image processing task (e.g., resizing and applying filters) to multiple AWS Lambda functions running in parallel. The fan-in pattern will aggregate the results of these functions.

Step 1: Upload Image Handler (Fan-Out)

The upload image handler receives the image and initiates the fan-out process by distributing the image processing tasks to multiple Lambda functions via an SQS queue.

```python
import json
import boto3

sqs = boto3.client('sqs')
processing_queue_url = 'your_processing_queue_url'

def lambda_handler(event, context):
    image_data = json.loads(event['body'])

    # Create processing tasks
    tasks = [
        {'task': 'resize', 'image': image_data},
        {'task': 'filter', 'image': image_data}
    ]
```

```
    # Send tasks to SQS queue
    for task in tasks:
        sqs.send_message(
            QueueUrl=processing_queue_url,
            MessageBody=json.dumps(task)
        )

    return {
        'statusCode': 200,
        'body': json.dumps('Image processing tasks created successfully')
    }
```

Step 2: Image Processing Worker (Fan-Out)

Each image processing worker function retrieves tasks from the SQS queue, processes the image (resizing or filtering), and stores the result.

```python
import json
import boto3

s3 = boto3.client('s3')
sqs = boto3.client('sqs')

def lambda_handler(event, context):
```

```python
    for record in event['Records']:
        task = json.loads(record['body'])
        image = task['image']

        if task['task'] == 'resize':
            result = resize_image(image)
        elif task['task'] == 'filter':
            result = apply_filter(image)

        # Store the processed image result in S3
        s3.put_object(
            Bucket='your_bucket_name',
            Key=f"{task['task']}_{image['id']}.jpg",
            Body=result
        )

        # Remove the processed message from the queue
        sqs.delete_message(
            QueueUrl='your_processing_queue_url',
            ReceiptHandle=record['receiptHandle']
        )

def resize_image(image):
    # Image resizing logic
    return b'resized_image_data'

def apply_filter(image):
    # Image filtering logic
```

```
    return b'filtered_image_data'
```

Step 3: Aggregation Handler (Fan-In)

The aggregation handler collects the results from S3 and aggregates them into a single response once all tasks are complete.

```python
import json
import boto3

s3 = boto3.client('s3')
sqs = boto3.client('sqs')
result_queue_url = 'your_result_queue_url'

def lambda_handler(event, context):
    for record in event['Records']:
        task = json.loads(record['body'])
        image_id = task['image']['id']

        # Aggregate results from S3
        resized_image = s3.get_object(Bucket='your_bucket_name', Key=f"resize_{image_id}.jpg")['Body'].read()
```

```python
        filtered_image = s3.get_object(Bucket='your_bucket_name', Key=f"filter_{image_id}.jpg")['Body'].read()

        # Combine results and store final output
        final_result = combine_images(resized_image, filtered_image)
        s3.put_object(
            Bucket='your_bucket_name',
            Key=f"final_{image_id}.jpg",
            Body=final_result
        )

        # Notify completion
        sqs.send_message(
            QueueUrl=result_queue_url,
            MessageBody=json.dumps({'status': 'complete', 'image_id': image_id})
        )

        # Remove the processed message from the queue
        sqs.delete_message(
            QueueUrl='your_processing_queue_url',
            ReceiptHandle=record['receiptHandle']
        )

def combine_images(resized_image, filtered_image):
    # Logic to combine resized and filtered images
```

```
    return b'final_combined_image_data'
```

Scalable Software Architecture Patterns

Microservices

Implementing the fan-out and fan-in patterns in a microservices architecture enables each service to focus on a specific task, such as resizing or filtering images. This modular approach enhances scalability, maintainability, and fault tolerance.

Example: Microservices for Image Processing

- **Upload Service**: Handles image uploads and initiates the fan-out process.

- **Resizing Service:** Processes image resizing tasks.

- **Filtering Service:** Processes image filtering tasks.

- **Aggregation Service:** Aggregates the results of image processing tasks.

Event-Driven Architecture

An event-driven architecture leverages events to trigger the fan-out and fan-in processes. This architecture ensures loose coupling between services and enables real-time processing and scalability.

Example: Event-Driven Image Processing Workflow

1. Image Uploaded Event: Triggers the creation of image processing tasks (fan-out).

2. Task Completed Event: Each processing task (resize or filter) publishes an event upon completion.

3. Aggregation Event: The final aggregation is triggered by the completion of all processing tasks (fan-in).

Best Practices for Implementing Fan-Out and Fan-In Patterns

1. Design for Idempotence: Ensure that tasks are idempotent, meaning they can be safely repeated without affecting the outcome. This is crucial for reliability and fault tolerance.

2. Implement Retry Mechanisms: Use automatic retries with exponential backoff for handling transient failures in task processing.

3. Use Dead-Letter Queues (DLQs): Configure DLQs to capture and analyze failed tasks, ensuring they do not get lost and can be addressed.

4. Monitor and Optimize: Continuously monitor the performance of the fan-out and fan-in processes and optimize for efficiency and scalability.

5. Ensure Security and Compliance: Secure data in transit and at rest, and ensure compliance with relevant regulations and standards.

Implementing the fan-out and fan-in patterns in serverless systems is a powerful approach to achieving high throughput, scalability, and resilience. By distributing tasks across multiple parallel processes and aggregating the results, these patterns enhance the efficiency and performance of data processing pipelines. Leveraging scalable software architecture patterns such as microservices and event-driven architecture further enhances the benefits, enabling systems to handle large volumes of data and react to changes in real-time. As organizations continue to adopt serverless computing, mastering the implementation of fan-out and fan-in patterns will be essential for delivering high-performance, scalable, and reliable applications in today's dynamic digital landscape.

Chapter 6

Microservices for Scalability and Maintainability: Breaking Down the Monolithic

Microservices Architecture: Decomposing Applications into Smaller Services

Microservices architecture is a design pattern that structures an application as a collection of loosely coupled services. This approach aims to address the limitations of monolithic architectures by decomposing applications into smaller, more manageable pieces that can be developed, deployed, and scaled independently.

Key Concepts of Microservices

1. Service Independence: Each microservice is a distinct entity that encapsulates its own data and logic.

2. Scalability: Services can be scaled independently to meet demand, improving resource utilization.

3. Flexibility: Different services can use different technologies, languages, and databases.

4. Resilience: Failures in one service do not necessarily affect others, enhancing overall system reliability.

5. Continuous Deployment: Services can be updated independently, enabling frequent and incremental updates.

Decomposing Applications into Microservices

The process of decomposing a monolithic application into microservices involves identifying distinct business capabilities and services that can function independently. For example, an e-commerce application can be broken down into the following microservices:

- **User Service:** Manages user authentication and profiles.

- **Product Service:** Handles product information and catalog management.

- Order Service: Manages order creation, processing, and tracking.

- **Payment Service:** Processes payments and manages billing.

Microservices Architecture Patterns

1. **API Gateway:** Acts as an entry point for clients to interact with the microservices, handling routing, composition, and protocol translation.

2. **Service Discovery**: Automates the detection of services and their instances, enabling dynamic scaling and load balancing.

3. **Circuit Breaker:** Prevents cascading failures by stopping calls to a failing service, allowing the system to degrade gracefully.

4. **Event-Driven Architecture:** Uses events to trigger actions and workflows across services, promoting loose coupling and asynchronous communication.

5. **Database per Service:** Each service manages its own database, ensuring data encapsulation and reducing the risk of cross-service data corruption.

Implementing Microservices with Serverless Technologies

Serverless computing, such as AWS Lambda, Google Cloud Functions, and Azure Functions, allows developers to run code without provisioning or managing servers. This complements microservices architecture by providing scalability, cost-efficiency, and ease of deployment.

Here's an example of how to implement a simple e-commerce application using AWS Lambda and API Gateway.

Step 1: Define Microservices

1. User Service (Python with AWS Lambda)

```python
import json
import boto3
from botocore.exceptions import ClientError

def lambda_handler(event, context):
    dynamodb = boto3.resource('dynamodb')
    table = dynamodb.Table('Users')

    if event['httpMethod'] == 'POST':
        try:
            data = json.loads(event['body'])
            response = table.put_item(Item=data)
            return {
                'statusCode': 200,
                'body': json.dumps({'message': 'User created successfully'})
```

```
        }
    except ClientError as e:
        return {
            'statusCode': 400,
            'body': json.dumps({'message': e.response['Error']['Message']})
        }
elif event['httpMethod'] == 'GET':
    user_id = event['queryStringParameters']['id']
    try:
        response = table.get_item(Key={'id': user_id})
        return {
            'statusCode': 200,
            'body': json.dumps(response['Item'])
        }
    except ClientError as e:
        return {
            'statusCode': 400,
            'body': json.dumps({'message': e.response['Error']['Message']})
        }
```

2. Product Service (Node.js with AWS Lambda)

```javascript
const AWS = require('aws-sdk');
```

```javascript
const docClient = new AWS.DynamoDB.DocumentClient();

exports.handler = async (event) => {
  if (event.httpMethod === 'POST') {
    const data = JSON.parse(event.body);
    const params = {
      TableName: 'Products',
      Item: data
    };
    try {
      await docClient.put(params).promise();
      return {
        statusCode: 200,
        body: JSON.stringify({ message: 'Product added successfully' })
      };
    } catch (err) {
      return {
        statusCode: 400,
        body: JSON.stringify({ message: err.message })
      };
    }
  } else if (event.httpMethod === 'GET') {
    const productId = event.queryStringParameters.id;
    const params = {
      TableName: 'Products',
```

```javascript
            Key: { id: productId }
        };
        try {
            const data = await docClient.get(params).promise();
            return {
                statusCode: 200,
                body: JSON.stringify(data.Item)
            };
        } catch (err) {
            return {
                statusCode: 400,
                body: JSON.stringify({ message: err.message })
            };
        };
```

3. Order Service (Python with AWS Lambda)

```python
import json
import boto3
from botocore.exceptions import ClientError

def lambda_handler(event, context):
    dynamodb = boto3.resource('dynamodb')
    table = dynamodb.Table('Orders')
```

```python
    if event['httpMethod'] == 'POST':
        try:
            data = json.loads(event['body'])
            response = table.put_item(Item=data)
            return {
                'statusCode': 200,
                'body': json.dumps({'message': 'Order placed successfully'})
            }
        except ClientError as e:
            return {
                'statusCode': 400,
                'body': json.dumps({'message': e.response['Error']['Message']})
            }
    elif event['httpMethod'] == 'GET':
        order_id = event['queryStringParameters']['id']
        try:
            response = table.get_item(Key={'id': order_id})
            return {
                'statusCode': 200,
                'body': json.dumps(response['Item'])
            }
        except ClientError as e:
            return {
                'statusCode': 400,
                'body': json.dumps({'message': e.response['Error']['Message']})
            }
```

}
```

## 4. Payment Service (Node.js with AWS Lambda)

```javascript
const stripe = require('stripe')(process.env.STRIPE_SECRET_KEY);

exports.handler = async (event) => {
  if (event.httpMethod === 'POST') {
    const data = JSON.parse(event.body);
    try {
      const paymentIntent = await stripe.paymentIntents.create({
        amount: data.amount,
        currency: 'usd',
        payment_method: data.payment_method_id,
        confirmation_method: 'manual',
        confirm: true,
      });
      return {
        statusCode: 200,
        body: JSON.stringify({ paymentIntent })
      };
    } catch (err) {
      return {
        statusCode: 400,

```
      body: JSON.stringify({ message:
err.message })
      };
```

Step 2: Configure API Gateway

- Create an API in API Gateway.

- Define routes for each microservice (e.g., `/users`, `/products`, `/orders`, `/payments`).

- Integrate each route with the corresponding Lambda function.

Step 3: Deploy the Services

- Deploy each Lambda function and API Gateway configuration.

- Ensure each service has appropriate IAM roles and permissions for accessing necessary AWS resources (e.g., DynamoDB, Stripe).

Step 4: Implement Service Discovery and Event-Driven Communication

- Use AWS Cloud Map for service discovery, enabling dynamic service registration and discovery.

- Implement AWS SNS or SQS for event-driven communication between microservices. For example, when an order is placed, the Order Service can publish an event to an SNS topic, which the Payment Service subscribes to for processing payments.

Scalable Patterns for Serverless Microservices

1. Database per Service: Ensures that each microservice has its own database, promoting data encapsulation and minimizing cross-service data dependencies.

2. Event-Driven Architecture: Uses events to trigger inter-service communication, reducing tight coupling and enhancing system flexibility.

3. Function Composition: Orchestrates multiple Lambda functions using AWS Step Functions, enabling complex workflows without tightly coupling services.

4. Asynchronous Messaging: Uses message queues (SQS) or pub/sub systems (SNS) to decouple services, improving scalability and resilience.

Best Practices for Microservices with Serverless

1. Statelessness: Ensure that each microservice is stateless, with no reliance on local state. Use databases or external storage for state persistence.

2. Resource Isolation: Allocate separate resources (e.g., DynamoDB tables, S3 buckets) for each microservice to avoid resource contention and data leakage.

3. Security: Implement fine-grained IAM policies for each Lambda function, restricting access to only the necessary resources.

4. Monitoring and Logging: Use AWS CloudWatch for monitoring and logging to gain insights into the performance and health of each service.

5. Error Handling and Retries: Implement robust error handling and retry mechanisms, particularly for communication between services.

Microservices architecture, combined with serverless technologies, offers a highly scalable, resilient, and flexible approach to building modern applications. By decomposing monolithic applications into smaller, independent services, organizations can achieve faster development cycles, better fault isolation, and more efficient resource utilization. Adopting best practices such as database per service, event-driven communication, and rigorous security measures ensures that the microservices architecture remains robust and maintainable.

Serverless Microservices: Leveraging the Benefits of Both Approaches

Serverless microservices combine two powerful architectural paradigms to create scalable, resilient, and efficient applications. By leveraging the strengths of serverless computing and microservices, organizations can build applications that are easier to develop, deploy, and manage. This approach enables on-demand scalability, cost efficiency, and reduced operational complexity.

Understanding Serverless and Microservices

Serverless Computing refers to the execution of code by a cloud provider without the need to manage the underlying infrastructure. Examples include AWS Lambda, Google Cloud Functions, and Azure Functions. Key benefits of serverless computing are:

- **Automatic scaling:** Resources automatically scale based on demand.

- **Cost efficiency:** You only pay for actual usage, not for idle resources.

- **Reduced operational overhead**: No need to provision, manage, or scale servers.

Microservices Architecture involves breaking down an application into smaller, loosely coupled services that can be developed, deployed, and scaled independently. Benefits include:

- **Modularity**: Easier maintenance and upgrades.

- **Scalability**: Each service can scale independently.

- **Flexibility**: Different services can use different technologies.

Combining these two approaches allows organizations to maximize the advantages of both, creating highly scalable and resilient systems.

Benefits of Combining Serverless and Microservices

1. Scalability: Serverless platforms automatically scale individual microservices based on demand, ensuring efficient resource utilization.

2. Cost Efficiency: With serverless, you only pay for what you use, making it cost-effective to run multiple microservices.

3. Reduced Complexity: Managing infrastructure becomes a non-issue, allowing developers to focus on writing code.

4. Faster Time to Market: Independent deployment and development cycles for each microservice enable quicker iterations and updates.

5. Improved Fault Isolation: Failures in one microservice do not impact others, enhancing the overall resilience of the application.

Designing Serverless Microservices

When designing serverless microservices, it's essential to follow best practices to ensure scalability, maintainability, and resilience.

Step 1: Define Microservices Boundaries

Start by identifying distinct business functionalities that can be developed as independent services. For example, in an e-commerce application:

- **User Service:** Manages user authentication and profiles.

- **Product Service:** Handles product catalog and details.
- **Order Service:** Manages order processing and tracking.

- **Payment Service:** Processes payments and handles billing.

Step 2: Implementing Serverless Microservices

Let's illustrate this with code examples using AWS Lambda and AWS API Gateway.

1. User Service (Python with AWS Lambda)

```python
import json
import boto3
from botocore.exceptions import ClientError
```

```python
def lambda_handler(event, context):
    dynamodb = boto3.resource('dynamodb')
    table = dynamodb.Table('Users')

    if event['httpMethod'] == 'POST':
        try:
            data = json.loads(event['body'])
            response = table.put_item(Item=data)
            return {
                'statusCode': 200,
                'body': json.dumps({'message': 'User created successfully'})
            }
        except ClientError as e:
            return {
                'statusCode': 400,
                'body': json.dumps({'message': e.response['Error']['Message']})
            }
    elif event['httpMethod'] == 'GET':
        user_id = event['queryStringParameters']['id']
        try:
            response = table.get_item(Key={'id': user_id})
            return {
                'statusCode': 200,
                'body': json.dumps(response['Item'])
            }
        except ClientError as e:
```

```
      return {
        'statusCode': 400,
        'body': json.dumps({'message':
e.response['Error']['Message']})
      }
```

2. Product Service (Node.js with AWS Lambda)

```javascript
const AWS = require('aws-sdk');
const docClient = new AWS.DynamoDB.DocumentClient();

exports.handler = async (event) => {
  if (event.httpMethod === 'POST') {
    const data = JSON.parse(event.body);
    const params = {
      TableName: 'Products',
      Item: data
    };
    try {
      await docClient.put(params).promise();
      return {
        statusCode: 200,
        body: JSON.stringify({ message: 'Product added successfully' })
      };
```

```
      } catch (err) {
        return {
          statusCode: 400,
          body: JSON.stringify({ message: err.message
        };
      }
    } else if (event.httpMethod === 'GET') {
      const productId = event.queryStringParameters.id;
      const params = {
        TableName: 'Products',
        Key: { id: productId }
      };
      try {
        const data = await docClient.get(params).promise();
        return {
          statusCode: 200,
          body: JSON.stringify(data.Item)
        };
      } catch (err) {
        return {
          statusCode: 400,
          body: JSON.stringify({ message: err.message
        };
```
```

## 3. Order Service (Python with AWS Lambda)
```

```python
import json
import boto3
from botocore.exceptions import ClientError

def lambda_handler(event, context):
    dynamodb = boto3.resource('dynamodb')
    table = dynamodb.Table('Orders')

    if event['httpMethod'] == 'POST':
        try:
            data = json.loads(event['body'])
            response = table.put_item(Item=data)
            return {
                'statusCode': 200,
                'body': json.dumps({'message': 'Order placed successfully'})
            }
        except ClientError as e:
            return {
                'statusCode': 400,
                'body': json.dumps({'message': e.response['Error']['Message']})
            }
    elif event['httpMethod'] == 'GET':
        order_id = event['queryStringParameters']['id']
        try:
            response = table.get_item(Key={'id': order_id})
```

```python
        return {
            'statusCode': 200,
            'body': json.dumps(response['Item'])
        }
    except ClientError as e:
        return {
            'statusCode': 400,
            'body': json.dumps({'message': e.response['Error']['Message']})
        }
```

4. Payment Service (Node.js with AWS Lambda)

```javascript
const stripe = require('stripe')(process.env.STRIPE_SECRET_KEY);

exports.handler = async (event) => {
    if (event.httpMethod === 'POST') {
        const data = JSON.parse(event.body);
        try {
            const paymentIntent = await stripe.paymentIntents.create({
                amount: data.amount,
                currency: 'usd',
                payment_method: data.payment_method_id,
                confirmation_method: 'manual',
```

```
        confirm: true,
      });
      return {
        statusCode: 200,
        body: JSON.stringify({ paymentIntent })
      };
    } catch (err) {
      return {
        statusCode: 400,
        body: JSON.stringify({ message: err.message
};
```

Step 3: Configuring API Gateway

- Create an API in API Gateway.

- Define routes for each microservice (e.g., `/users`, `/products`, `/orders`, `/payments`).

- Integrate each route with the corresponding Lambda function.

Step 4: Deploying the Services

- Deploy each Lambda function and configure API Gateway.

- Ensure each service has appropriate IAM roles and permissions to access necessary AWS resources (e.g., DynamoDB, Stripe).

Step 5: Implementing Event-Driven Communication

Use AWS services like SNS (Simple Notification Service) or SQS (Simple Queue Service) for event-driven communication between microservices.

1. Order Service Publishes Event to SNS

```python
import json
import boto3

def lambda_handler(event, context):
    sns = boto3.client('sns')
    order_data = json.loads(event['body'])

    response = sns.publish(
        TopicArn='arn:aws:sns:region:account-id:order-topic',
        Message=json.dumps(order_data),
        Subject='New Order Placed'
    )

    return {
```

```
        'statusCode': 200,
        'body': json.dumps({'message': 'Order placed and notification sent'})
    }
```

2. Payment Service Subscribes to SNS Topic

```javascript
const AWS = require('aws-sdk');
const stripe = require('stripe')(process.env.STRIPE_SECRET_KEY);

exports.handler = async (event) => {
    const snsMessage = event.Records[0].Sns.Message;
    const orderData = JSON.parse(snsMessage);

    try {
        const paymentIntent = await stripe.paymentIntents.create({
            amount: orderData.amount,
            currency: 'usd',
            payment_method: orderData.payment_method_id,
            confirmation_method: 'manual',
            confirm: true,
        });
        return {
```

```
      statusCode: 200,
      body: JSON.stringify({ paymentIntent })
    };
  } catch (err) {
    return {
      statusCode: 400,
      body: JSON.stringify({ message: err.message })
    };
```
```

## Scalable Patterns for Serverless Microservices

**1. Database per Service:** Ensure each microservice has its own database to maintain data encapsulation and reduce coupling.

**2. Event-Driven Architecture:** Utilize events to trigger actions and workflows across services, promoting loose coupling and asynchronous communication.

**3. Function Composition:** Use orchestration tools like AWS Step Functions to manage complex workflows across multiple Lambda functions.

**4. Asynchronous Messaging:** Use SQS or SNS to decouple services and handle asynchronous communication, improving scalability and resilience.
```

5. API Gateway: Use API Gateway as the entry point for all client requests. It handles request routing, throttling, and security, ensuring a clean separation between client-facing APIs and backend microservices.

6. Security and IAM Policies: Implement fine-grained IAM policies to restrict each microservice's access to only the resources it needs, ensuring the principle of least privilege.

7. Monitoring and Logging: Use AWS CloudWatch for centralized logging, metrics, and monitoring to gain insights into the health and performance of each microservice.

Best Practices for Serverless Microservices

1. Statelessness: Ensure that each Lambda function is stateless, meaning it doesn't rely on local state. Use external storage (e.g., databases, S3) to persist data.

2. Granular Functions: Keep Lambda functions small and focused on a single responsibility. This promotes modularity and makes the code easier to understand and maintain.

3. Environment Variables: Use environment variables to manage configuration settings, such as database connection strings and API keys. This avoids hard-coding sensitive information.

4. Cold Start Optimization: To mitigate cold start latency, especially in critical paths, consider using provisioned concurrency for Lambda functions that require high availability.

5. Efficient Error Handling: Implement robust error handling and retries in your Lambda functions. AWS Lambda has built-in support for retries on failure, but handling errors gracefully within the code is crucial.

6. Testing and CI/CD: Implement automated testing and continuous integration/continuous deployment (CI/CD) pipelines. Tools like AWS CodePipeline and AWS CodeBuild can streamline the deployment process.

Example: Implementing a Serverless Microservices Architecture

Let's put everything together with a simplified example of an e-commerce platform. We'll use AWS services to demonstrate a complete flow from API Gateway to Lambda functions and DynamoDB.

User Service

```python
# User Service Lambda (Python)
import json
import boto3
from botocore.exceptions import ClientError

def lambda_handler(event, context):
    dynamodb = boto3.resource('dynamodb')
    table = dynamodb.Table('Users')

    if event['httpMethod'] == 'POST':
        try:
            data = json.loads(event['body'])
            response = table.put_item(Item=data)
            return {
                'statusCode': 200,
                'body': json.dumps({'message': 'User created successfully'})
            }
        except ClientError as e:
            return {
                'statusCode': 400,
                'body': json.dumps({'message': e.response['Error']['Message']})
            }
    elif event['httpMethod'] == 'GET':
        user_id = event['queryStringParameters']['id']
        try:
```

```python
        response = table.get_item(Key={'id': user_id})
        return {
            'statusCode': 200,
            'body': json.dumps(response['Item'])
        }
    except ClientError as e:
        return {
            'statusCode': 400,
            'body': json.dumps({'message': e.response['Error']['Message']})
        }
```

Product Service

```javascript
// Product Service Lambda (Node.js)
const AWS = require('aws-sdk');
const docClient = new AWS.DynamoDB.DocumentClient();

exports.handler = async (event) => {
  if (event.httpMethod === 'POST') {
    const data = JSON.parse(event.body);
    const params = {
      TableName: 'Products',
      Item: data
    };
```

```
        try {
            await docClient.put(params).promise();
            return {
                statusCode: 200,
                body: JSON.stringify({ message: 'Product added successfully' })
            };
        } catch (err) {
            return {
                statusCode: 400,
                body: JSON.stringify({ message: err.message
            };
        }
    } else if (event.httpMethod === 'GET') {
        const productId = event.queryStringParameters.id;
        const params = {
            TableName: 'Products',
            Key: { id: productId }
        };
        try {
            const data = await docClient.get(params).promise();
            return {
                statusCode: 200,
                body: JSON.stringify(data.Item)
            };
        } catch (err) {
            return {
```

```
      statusCode: 400,
      body: JSON.stringify({ message: err.message
   };
```

Order Service

```python
# Order Service Lambda (Python)
import json
import boto3
from botocore.exceptions import ClientError

def lambda_handler(event, context):
    dynamodb = boto3.resource('dynamodb')
    table = dynamodb.Table('Orders')
    sns = boto3.client('sns')

    if event['httpMethod'] == 'POST':
        try:
            data = json.loads(event['body'])
            response = table.put_item(Item=data)

            sns.publish(
                TopicArn='arn:aws:sns:region:account-id:order-topic',
                Message=json.dumps(data),
                Subject='New Order Placed'
```

```
            )

        return {
            'statusCode': 200,
            'body': json.dumps({'message': 'Order placed successfully and notification sent'})
        }
    except ClientError as e:
        return {
            'statusCode': 400,
            'body': json.dumps({'message': e.response['Error']['Message']})
        }
  elif event['httpMethod'] == 'GET':
    order_id = event['queryStringParameters']['id']
    try:
        response = table.get_item(Key={'id': order_id})
        return {
            'statusCode': 200,
            'body': json.dumps(response['Item'])
        }
    except ClientError as e:
        return {
            'statusCode': 400,
            'body': json.dumps({'message': e.response['Error']['Message']})
        }
```

Payment Service

```javascript
// Payment Service Lambda (Node.js)
const AWS = require('aws-sdk');
const stripe = require('stripe')(process.env.STRIPE_SECRET_KEY);

exports.handler = async (event) => {
  const snsMessage = event.Records[0].Sns.Message;
  const orderData = JSON.parse(snsMessage);

  try {
    const paymentIntent = await stripe.paymentIntents.create({
        amount: orderData.amount,
        currency: 'usd',
        payment_method: orderData.payment_method_id,
        confirmation_method: 'manual',
        confirm: true,
    });
    return {
      statusCode: 200,
      body: JSON.stringify({ paymentIntent })
    };
  } catch (err) {
```

```
    return {
      statusCode: 400,
      body: JSON.stringify({ message: err.message })
    };
```

Deploying the Architecture

1. Create DynamoDB Tables: Create DynamoDB tables for Users, Products, and Orders.

2. Deploy Lambda Functions: Deploy the Lambda functions for User Service, Product Service, Order Service, and Payment Service.

3. Configure API Gateway: Set up API Gateway with routes for each service and integrate them with the corresponding Lambda functions.

4. Set Up SNS: Create an SNS topic for order notifications and subscribe the Payment Service Lambda to this topic.

5. Environment Variables: Configure environment variables for your Lambda functions, such as the Stripe API key and SNS topic ARN.

Combining serverless computing with microservices architecture provides a powerful framework for building scalable, resilient, and cost-efficient applications. By decomposing your application into smaller, independent services and leveraging serverless technologies, you can achieve greater flexibility, faster time to market, and improved fault isolation. Implementing best practices such as statelessness, fine-grained IAM policies, and efficient error handling will ensure your serverless microservices architecture remains robust and maintainable.

Serverless microservices are particularly well-suited for dynamic, high-growth environments where scalability and agility are paramount. By embracing this architectural approach, organizations can stay competitive and responsive to ever-changing business needs while optimizing their operational costs and infrastructure management efforts.

Designing Microservices Boundaries for Scalability and Loose Coupling

In the rapidly evolving landscape of software architecture, microservices have emerged as a pivotal approach to building scalable and resilient systems. This architectural style involves decomposing a monolithic application into smaller, independent services that can be developed, deployed, and scaled individually. A critical aspect of designing microservices is establishing appropriate boundaries that promote scalability and loose coupling. In this discussion, we will explore strategies for defining these boundaries, supported by code examples and principles from scalable software architecture patterns, particularly for serverless systems.

Principles of Microservices Boundaries

1. Single Responsibility Principle (SRP): Each microservice should have a well-defined responsibility. This principle ensures that services are cohesive and focused, making them easier to manage and scale.

2. Domain-Driven Design (DDD): Using DDD to identify bounded contexts helps in defining service boundaries that align with business domains. This alignment ensures that services encapsulate domain logic effectively and are loosely coupled with other services.

3. Independent Scalability: Microservices should be designed to scale independently based on their specific resource requirements and usage patterns. This requires careful consideration of how services interact and share data.

4. Loose Coupling and High Cohesion: Services should minimize dependencies on other services. Loose coupling ensures that changes in one service do not impact others, while high cohesion ensures that related functionalities are encapsulated within the same service.

Designing Boundaries with Domain-Driven Design

Domain-Driven Design (DDD) provides a strategic approach to defining microservices boundaries by focusing on the business domain. The core concept in DDD is the bounded context, which represents a boundary within which a particular model is defined and applicable.

Consider an e-commerce platform with the following high-level domains:

- **User Management:** Handles user registration, authentication, and profile management.

- **Product Catalog:** Manages product listings, categories, and inventory.

- **Order Processing:** Manages orders, payments, and shipping.

- **Notification Service:** Handles sending notifications (e.g., emails, SMS).

Each of these domains can be mapped to a microservice. Let's look at how we can design these boundaries using DDD and serverless architecture.

Example: User Management Service

```python
# User Management Service using AWS Lambda and DynamoDB

import json
import boto3
from botocore.exceptions import ClientError

dynamodb = boto3.resource('dynamodb')
table = dynamodb.Table('Users')

def lambda_handler(event, context):
    operation = event.get('operation')

    if operation == 'createUser':
        return create_user(event['payload'])
    elif operation == 'getUser':
        return get_user(event['payload'])
    elif operation == 'updateUser':
        return update_user(event['payload'])
    elif operation == 'deleteUser':
        return delete_user(event['payload'])
```

```python
    else:
        return {"error": "Unsupported operation"}

def create_user(user_data):
    try:
        table.put_item(Item=user_data)
        return {"message": "User created successfully"}
    except ClientError as e:
        return {"error": str(e)}

def get_user(user_id):
    try:
        response = table.get_item(Key={'userId': user_id})
        if 'Item' in response:
            return response['Item']
        else:
            return {"error": "User not found"}
    except ClientError as e:
        return {"error": str(e)}

def update_user(user_data):
    try:
        response = table.update_item(
            Key={'userId': user_data['userId']},
            UpdateExpression="set info=:i",
            ExpressionAttributeValues={
                ':i': user_data['info']
            },
```

```
        ReturnValues="UPDATED_NEW"
    )
    return {"message": "User updated successfully"}
except ClientError as e:
    return {"error": str(e)}

def delete_user(user_id):
    try:
        table.delete_item(Key={'userId': user_id})
        return {"message": "User deleted successfully"}
    except ClientError as e:
        return {"error": str(e)}
```

In this example, the `User Management Service` is implemented as an AWS Lambda function that interacts with DynamoDB for persistence. Each operation (create, read, update, delete) is encapsulated within the service, ensuring it adheres to SRP.

Communication Between Microservices

To maintain loose coupling, microservices should communicate asynchronously wherever possible. This can be achieved using messaging systems like Amazon SQS (Simple Queue Service) or SNS (Simple Notification Service).

```python
# Order Processing Service sending notification using SNS

import json
import boto3
from botocore.exceptions import ClientError

sns = boto3.client('sns')

def lambda_handler(event, context):
    operation = event.get('operation')

    if operation == 'createOrder':
        return create_order(event['payload'])
    else:
        return {"error": "Unsupported operation"}

def create_order(order_data):
    # Logic to create an order (omitted for brevity)
    send_notification(order_data)
    return {"message": "Order created successfully"}

def send_notification(order_data):
    try:
        response = sns.publish(
            TopicArn='arn:aws:sns:region:account-id:OrderNotifications',
```

```
        Message=json.dumps({'default':
json.dumps(order_data)}),
        MessageStructure='json'
    )
    return {"message": "Notification sent successfully"}
  except ClientError as e:
    return {"error": str(e)}
```

In this example, the `Order Processing Service` publishes a message to an SNS topic whenever a new order is created. The `Notification Service` can subscribe to this topic to handle the notification logic, thereby decoupling the order processing logic from the notification logic.

Event-Driven Architecture

Using an event-driven architecture can further enhance the scalability and loose coupling of microservices. Events represent significant changes or actions within a system, and services can react to these events as needed.

For instance, in an e-commerce platform, an `OrderPlaced` event can be emitted when a new order is created. Various services like inventory management, shipping, and notifications can subscribe to this event and perform their respective tasks.

```python
# OrderPlaced Event Publisher

import json
import boto3
from botocore.exceptions import ClientError

eventbridge = boto3.client('events')

def publish_order_placed_event(order_data):
    try:
        response = eventbridge.put_events(
            Entries=[
                {
                    'Source': 'com.mycompany.orders',
                    'DetailType': 'OrderPlaced',
                    'Detail': json.dumps(order_data),
                    'EventBusName': 'default'
                }
            ]
        return {"message": "OrderPlaced event published successfully"}
    except ClientError as e:
        return {"error": str(e)}
```

In this example, the `OrderPlaced` event is published to Amazon EventBridge, which then routes the event to any interested subscribers.

Managing Data Consistency

One of the challenges with microservices is managing data consistency, especially in distributed systems. Using patterns like the Saga pattern can help coordinate complex transactions across multiple services.

Saga Pattern: A saga is a sequence of local transactions where each transaction updates the database and publishes an event or message. If a step fails, compensating transactions are executed to undo the previous steps.

```python
# Simplified example of a Saga using AWS Step Functions

import json
import boto3

stepfunctions = boto3.client('stepfunctions')

def lambda_handler(event, context):
    order_data = event['order_data']
```

```
    response = start_saga(order_data)
    return response

def start_saga(order_data):
    try:
        response = stepfunctions.start_execution(
            stateMachineArn='arn:aws:states:region:account-id:stateMachine:OrderSaga',
            input=json.dumps(order_data)
        )
        return {"message": "Saga started successfully"}
    except ClientError as e:
        return {"error": str(e)}
```

In this example, an AWS Step Functions state machine orchestrates the Saga, ensuring that each step in the order processing workflow is executed and, if necessary, rolled back.

Designing microservices boundaries for scalability and loose coupling involves careful consideration of domain-driven design principles, independent scalability, and the use of asynchronous communication and event-driven architectures. By adhering to these principles and leveraging serverless technologies, we can build robust, scalable, and maintainable systems.

The provided examples illustrate how to implement microservices in a serverless environment using AWS Lambda, DynamoDB, SNS, EventBridge, and Step Functions. These patterns and practices ensure that microservices remain loosely coupled and scalable, allowing for the independent evolution of services and the ability to handle varying loads effectively.

Chapter 7

Understanding Caching: Optimizing Performance and Reducing Costs

Caching is a fundamental technique for optimizing performance and reducing costs in software systems. By temporarily storing frequently accessed data in a cache, systems can respond to requests faster and reduce the load on underlying data sources. This is especially crucial in serverless architectures, where optimizing resource usage directly impacts cost efficiency. In this discussion, we'll explore the principles of caching, supported by code examples and scalable software architecture patterns tailored for serverless systems.

Principles of Caching

1. Temporal Locality: Temporal locality refers to the concept that recently accessed data is likely to be accessed again. Caching capitalizes on this by storing recently used data close to where it is needed.

2. Spatial Locality: Spatial locality means that data elements close to each other are likely to be accessed together. Caching data in chunks or pages can exploit this principle.

3. Cache Invalidation: Managing the cache lifecycle, including invalidation strategies, ensures data consistency. Common strategies include time-to-live (TTL), manual invalidation, and event-based invalidation.

4. Cache Hit and Miss: A cache hit occurs when requested data is found in the cache, while a cache miss happens when it is not. Optimizing for a high cache hit rate is key to effective caching.

5. Eviction Policies: Eviction policies determine which data to remove from the cache when it reaches capacity. Common policies include Least Recently Used (LRU), Most Recently Used (MRU), and Least Frequently Used (LFU).

Implementing Caching in Serverless Systems

Serverless architectures, such as those built on AWS Lambda, offer unique opportunities and challenges for implementing caching. Let's look at how to apply caching effectively in a serverless context using AWS services like AWS Lambda, Amazon DynamoDB, and Amazon ElastiCache.

Example: Caching with AWS Lambda and Amazon ElastiCache

Consider a scenario where an application frequently queries user profile data stored in Amazon DynamoDB. To optimize performance and reduce DynamoDB read costs, we can cache user profile data using Amazon ElastiCache with Redis.

1. Setting Up ElastiCache (Redis): First, we need to set up an ElastiCache cluster with Redis.

```bash
aws elasticache create-cache-cluster \
    --cache-cluster-id my-redis-cluster \
    --engine redis \
    --cache-node-type cache.t2.micro \
    --num-cache-nodes 1
```

2. AWS Lambda Function with Caching: Here's a Lambda function that checks Redis for cached user profile data before querying DynamoDB.

```python
import json
import boto3
import redis
from botocore.exceptions import ClientError
```

```python
# Initialize DynamoDB and Redis clients
dynamodb = boto3.resource('dynamodb')
table = dynamodb.Table('Users')

redis_client = redis.StrictRedis(
    host='my-redis-cluster.xxxxxx.0001.use1.cache.amazonaws.com',
    port=6379,
    db=0,
    decode_responses=True
)

def lambda_handler(event, context):
    user_id = event['userId']
    profile_data = get_user_profile(user_id)
    return profile_data

def get_user_profile(user_id):
    # Check Redis cache first
    cached_data = redis_client.get(user_id)
    if cached_data:
        return json.loads(cached_data)

    # If not in cache, query DynamoDB
    try:
        response = table.get_item(Key={'userId': user_id})
        if 'Item' in response:
```

```
        profile_data = response['Item']
        # Store in cache with TTL of 3600 seconds (1 hour)
        redis_client.setex(user_id, 3600, json.dumps(profile_data))
        return profile_data
    else:
        return {"error": "User not found"}
  except ClientError as e:
    return {"error": str(e)}
```

In this example, the Lambda function first attempts to retrieve the user profile data from Redis. If the data is not in the cache (cache miss), it queries DynamoDB, stores the result in Redis with a TTL of one hour, and then returns the data.

Cache Invalidation Strategies

Proper cache invalidation is crucial for maintaining data consistency. Here are common strategies:

1. Time-to-Live (TTL): Setting an expiration time for cached items ensures they are refreshed periodically.

```python
```

```python
redis_client.setex(user_id, 3600, json.dumps(profile_data))
```

2. Manual Invalidation: Explicitly invalidating cache entries when data changes.

```python
redis_client.delete(user_id)
```

3. Event-Based Invalidatio: Using events to trigger cache invalidation. For instance, integrating with DynamoDB Streams to invalidate cache entries when the underlying data changes.

```python
# Lambda function to handle DynamoDB Streams and invalidate cache
def stream_handler(event, context):
    for record in event['Records']:
        if record['eventName'] == 'MODIFY':
            user_id = record['dynamodb']['Keys']['userId']['S']
            redis_client.delete(user_id)
```

This Lambda function listens to changes in the DynamoDB table and invalidates the corresponding cache entries.

Caching Patterns for Serverless Architectures

1. Read-Through Cache: The application queries the cache first and, on a miss, retrieves data from the database, updates the cache, and returns the data.

```python
def read_through_cache(key):
    value = redis_client.get(key)
    if not value:
        value = query_database(key)
        redis_client.set(key, value)
    return value
```

2. Write-Through Cache: Writes go through the cache, ensuring that both the cache and the database are updated simultaneously.

```python
def write_through_cache(key, value):
    redis_client.set(key, value)
    update_database(key, value)
```

3. Cache-Aside: The application manages the cache explicitly, querying the database directly on a cache miss and updating the cache as needed.

```python
def cache_aside(key):
    value = redis_client.get(key)
    if not value:
        value = query_database(key)
        redis_client.set(key, value)
    return value
```

4. Write-Around Cache: Writes bypass the cache and go directly to the database. The cache is updated only on subsequent reads.

```python
def write_around_cache(key, value):
    update_database(key, value)
    # Cache will be updated on next read
```

Cost Optimization through Caching

Caching not only improves performance but also helps in reducing costs, especially in serverless environments where costs are usage-based.

1. Reduced Database Load: By serving frequent read requests from the cache, the load on databases like DynamoDB is significantly reduced, leading to lower read operation costs.

```python
def get_user_profile(user_id):
    cached_data = redis_client.get(user_id)
    if cached_data:
        return json.loads(cached_data)
    # Database read happens only on cache miss
    response = table.get_item(Key={'userId': user_id})
    profile_data = response['Item']
    redis_client.setex(user_id, 3600, json.dumps(profile_data))
    return profile_data
```

2. Optimized Lambda Execution Time: Since cache access is typically faster than database queries, the overall execution time of Lambda functions is reduced, leading to lower Lambda invocation costs.

3. Efficient Use of Serverless Compute Resources: By reducing the time spent waiting for database responses, serverless functions can handle more requests within the same period, improving resource utilization.

Monitoring and Metrics

Effective caching also involves monitoring cache performance and utilization. Key metrics to track include:

1. Cache Hit Rate: The ratio of cache hits to total cache accesses. A high hit rate indicates effective caching.

```python
cache_hits = 0
cache_misses = 0

def get_user_profile(user_id):
    global cache_hits, cache_misses
    cached_data = redis_client.get(user_id)
    if cached_data:
        cache_hits += 1
        return json.loads(cached_data)
    else:
        cache_misses += 1
        response = table.get_item(Key={'userId': user_id})
```

```
        profile_data = response['Item']
        redis_client.setex(user_id, 3600, json.dumps(profile_data))
        return profile_data

    def get_cache_metrics():
        total_requests = cache_hits + cache_misses
        hit_rate = cache_hits / total_requests if total_requests else 0
        return {"cache_hits": cache_hits, "cache_misses": cache_misses, "hit_rate": hit_rate}
```

2. Eviction Rate: The frequency at which items are evicted from the cache. Monitoring eviction helps in adjusting cache size and eviction policies.

3. Latency: Measuring the time taken to retrieve data from the cache versus the database helps in evaluating the performance benefits of caching.

Caching is an indispensable technique for optimizing performance and reducing costs in serverless architectures. By strategically caching frequently accessed data, we can minimize database load, reduce response times, and lower operational costs. The examples and patterns discussed, such as read-through, write-through, cache-aside, and write-around, illustrate various approaches to implementing caching effectively.

Using AWS services like Lambda, DynamoDB, and ElastiCache, we can build scalable and efficient serverless applications. Proper cache management, including invalidation strategies and monitoring, is crucial for maintaining the effectiveness and consistency of the cache. Here's a deeper dive into some of these aspects:

Advanced Cache Management

1. Cache Warming: To avoid cold starts where the cache is empty, cache warming can pre-populate the cache with frequently accessed data or critical information during deployment or startup phases. This ensures that the cache is ready to serve requests immediately.

```python
def warm_cache():
    popular_user_ids = get_popular_user_ids()
    for user_id in popular_user_ids:
        user_data = query_database(user_id)
        redis_client.setex(user_id, 3600, json.dumps(user_data))
```

```python
def get_popular_user_ids():
    # Logic to fetch popular user IDs
    return ["user1", "user2", "user3"]
```

2. Cache Refresh: Regularly refreshing cache entries ensures that stale data is minimized. This can be done through background jobs or triggered functions that periodically update the cache.

```python
import schedule
import time

def refresh_cache():
    user_ids = get_all_user_ids()
    for user_id in user_ids:
        user_data = query_database(user_id)
        redis_client.setex(user_id, 3600, json.dumps(user_data))

# Schedule the cache refresh job to run every hour
schedule.every().hour.do(refresh_cache)

while True:
    schedule.run_pending()
    time.sleep(1)
```

3. Cache Metrics and Alerts*: Monitoring tools like Amazon CloudWatch can be integrated with Redis and Lambda to track metrics such as cache hits, misses, latency, and eviction rates. Setting up alerts on these metrics helps in proactive cache management.

```python
import boto3

cloudwatch = boto3.client('cloudwatch')

def publish_cache_metrics():
    total_requests = cache_hits + cache_misses
    hit_rate = cache_hits / total_requests if total_requests else 0

    cloudwatch.put_metric_data(
        Namespace='MyApplication/Cache',
        MetricData=[
            {
                'MetricName': 'CacheHitRate',
                'Dimensions': [
                    {
                        'Name': 'Cache',
                        'Value': 'Redis'
                    },
```

```
            'Value': hit_rate,
            'Unit': 'Percent'
        },

# Call this function periodically to publish metrics
```

Example Use Case: E-commerce Product Catalog

In an e-commerce application, the product catalog is frequently accessed data that benefits significantly from caching. Here's how to implement caching for product details using AWS Lambda and Redis.

1. Lambda Function to Fetch Product Details:

```python
import json
import boto3
import redis

# Initialize DynamoDB and Redis clients
dynamodb = boto3.resource('dynamodb')
table = dynamodb.Table('Products')

redis_client = redis.StrictRedis(
    host='my-redis-cluster.xxxxxx.0001.use1.cache.amazonaws.com',
```

```python
    port=6379,
    db=0,
    decode_responses=True
)

def lambda_handler(event, context):
    product_id = event['productId']
    product_data = get_product_details(product_id)
    return product_data

def get_product_details(product_id):
    # Check Redis cache first
    cached_data = redis_client.get(product_id)
    if cached_data:
        return json.loads(cached_data)

    # If not in cache, query DynamoDB
    try:
        response = table.get_item(Key={'productId': product_id})
        if 'Item' in response:
            product_data = response['Item']
            # Store in cache with TTL of 3600 seconds (1 hour)
            redis_client.setex(product_id, 3600, json.dumps(product_data))
            return product_data
        else:
```

```
        return {"error": "Product not found"}
    except ClientError as e:
        return {"error": str(e)}
```

2. Manual Invalidation upon Product Update:

```python
def update_product(product_id, product_data):
    # Update the product in DynamoDB
    try:
        table.update_item(
            Key={'productId': product_id},
            UpdateExpression="set info=:i",
            ExpressionAttributeValues={
                ':i': product_data['info']
            },
            ReturnValues="UPDATED_NEW"
        )
        # Invalidate the cache entry
        redis_client.delete(product_id)
        return {"message": "Product updated successfully"}
    except ClientError as e:
        return {"error": str(e)}
```

3. Event-Based Invalidation with DynamoDB Streams:

```python
def stream_handler(event, context):
    for record in event['Records']:
        if record['eventName'] in ['MODIFY', 'REMOVE']:
            product_id = record['dynamodb']['Keys']['productId']['S']
            redis_client.delete(product_id)
```

By integrating DynamoDB Streams, any updates or deletions to product entries trigger the invalidation of the corresponding cache entries, ensuring data consistency.

Caching is a powerful strategy for enhancing performance and reducing costs in serverless architectures. By leveraging caching principles such as temporal locality, cache invalidation, and eviction policies, systems can handle high traffic efficiently and minimize latency.

In serverless environments, tools like AWS Lambda, DynamoDB, and ElastiCache (Redis) offer scalable solutions for implementing effective caching strategies. Through practical examples and patterns, we have explored how to cache data, manage cache lifecycles, and monitor performance to achieve optimal results.

Effective cache management ensures that serverless applications remain responsive, cost-effective, and capable of scaling to meet demand. By understanding and implementing the discussed caching techniques, developers can significantly improve the performance and efficiency of their serverless applications.

Implementing Caching at the Edge and Application Layers

Implementing caching at both the edge and application layers is crucial for building scalable and high-performing serverless systems. Caching reduces latency, decreases load on the backend, and improves the overall user experience. This guide will discuss caching strategies, focusing on scalable software architecture patterns, and provide code examples to illustrate key concepts.

Edge Caching

Edge caching refers to storing data closer to the end users, typically in a Content Delivery Network (CDN). This reduces the distance data needs to travel, thus decreasing latency.

Benefits of Edge Caching

- **Reduced Latency:** Data is served from a location closer to the user.

- **Offloaded Traffic:** Reduces the load on the origin server.

- **Improved Reliability:** Redundant cache locations can provide high availability.

Implementation with AWS CloudFront

AWS CloudFront is a widely used CDN that integrates well with other AWS services. Below is an example of setting up CloudFront for caching static assets and API responses.

Step 1: Create an S3 Bucket for Static Assets

```bash
aws s3 mb s3://my-static-assets
aws s3 cp --recursive ./static s3://my-static-assets
```

Step 2: Configure CloudFront Distribution

```python
```

```python
import boto3

client = boto3.client('cloudfront')

response = client.create_distribution(
    DistributionConfig={
        'CallerReference': 'unique-string',
        'Origins': {
            'Items': [
                {
                    'Id': 'S3-my-static-assets',
                    'DomainName': 'my-static-assets.s3.amazonaws.com',
                    'S3OriginConfig': {
                        'OriginAccessIdentity': ''
                    }

                    'Id': 'Custom-my-api',
                    'DomainName': 'api.example.com',
                    'CustomOriginConfig': {
                        'HTTPPort': 80,
                        'HTTPSPort': 443,
                        'OriginProtocolPolicy': 'https-only'
                    }

            'Quantity': 2
        },
        'DefaultCacheBehavior': {
```

```
        'TargetOriginId': 'S3-my-static-assets',
        'ViewerProtocolPolicy': 'redirect-to-https',
        'AllowedMethods': {
            'Items': ['GET', 'HEAD'],
            'Quantity': 2
        },
        'CachedMethods': {
            'Items': ['GET', 'HEAD'],
            'Quantity': 2
        },
        'ForwardedValues': {
            'QueryString': False,
            'Cookies': {'Forward': 'none'}
        },
        'MinTTL': 3600,
        'DefaultTTL': 86400,
        'MaxTTL': 31536000
    },
    'Comment': 'My CloudFront Distribution',
    'Enabled': True
}
```

Step 3: Invalidate Cache When Necessary

When assets are updated, the CDN cache should be invalidated to ensure users get the latest version.

```python
response = client.create_invalidation(
    DistributionId='EXXXXXXXXXXXX',
    InvalidationBatch={
        'Paths': {
            'Quantity': 1,
            'Items': ['/*']
        },
        'CallerReference': 'unique-string'
    }
)
```

Application Layer Caching

Application layer caching involves storing data closer to the application logic to reduce the need for repetitive data fetching or computations.

Benefits of Application Layer Caching

- **Reduced Database Load:** Less frequent database queries.

- **Faster Response Times:** Cached data can be returned immediately.

- **Cost Efficiency:** Reduced computational and data transfer costs.

Implementation with AWS Lambda and Redis (ElastiCache)

In a serverless architecture, AWS Lambda can be paired with a caching layer like Redis using AWS ElastiCache.

Step 1: Set Up Redis (ElastiCache)

```bash
aws elasticache create-cache-cluster \
    --cache-cluster-id my-redis-cluster \
    --engine redis \
    --cache-node-type cache.t2.micro \
    --num-cache-nodes 1
```

Step 2: Lambda Function to Use Redis Cache

```python
import json
import redis
import os

redis_host = os.environ.get('REDIS_HOST')

def lambda_handler(event, context):
```

```python
    r = redis.StrictRedis(host=redis_host, port=6379, db=0)

    cache_key = f"user:{event['user_id']}"
    user_data = r.get(cache_key)

    if user_data:
        return {
            'statusCode': 200,
            'body': json.dumps({'source': 'cache', 'data': json.loads(user_data)})
        }

    # Fetch from database (simulated)
    user_data = fetch_user_from_db(event['user_id'])

    # Cache the data
    r.setex(cache_key, 3600, json.dumps(user_data))

    return {
        'statusCode': 200,
        'body': json.dumps({'source': 'database', 'data': user_data})
    }

def fetch_user_from_db(user_id):
    # Simulate database fetch
    return {
```

```
        'user_id': user_id,
        'name': 'John Doe',
        'email': 'john.doe@example.com'
    }
```

Step 3: Environment Variables and IAM Roles

Ensure the Lambda function has the necessary environment variables set for the Redis host and the appropriate IAM role permissions to access ElastiCache.

```yaml
Resources:
  MyLambdaFunction:
    Type: AWS::Lambda::Function
    Properties:
      Handler: index.lambda_handler
      Runtime: python3.8
      Environment:
        Variables:
          REDIS_HOST: !Ref RedisEndpoint
      Role: !GetAtt LambdaExecutionRole.Arn

  RedisEndpoint:
    Type: "AWS::SSM::Parameter::Value<String>"
    Default: "/elasticache/my-redis-cluster/endpoint"
```

Scalable Architecture Patterns

For serverless systems, certain architecture patterns enhance scalability and performance.

1. Microservices with Caching

Each microservice can have its own cache layer. This approach isolates caches, reducing contention and improving scalability.

2. Event-Driven Cache Invalidation

Using AWS SNS or SQS, cache invalidation can be managed through events. For example, a database update can trigger an event that invalidates or updates the relevant cache entries.

```python
import boto3
import redis
import json

sns = boto3.client('sns')
redis_host = 'redis-endpoint'

def lambda_handler(event, context):
```

```
    r = redis.StrictRedis(host=redis_host, port=6379, db=0)

    # Invalidate cache upon receiving the event
    for record in event['Records']:
        message = json.loads(record['Sns']['Message'])
        if message['event_type'] == 'USER_UPDATE':
            cache_key = f"user:{message['user_id']}"
            r.delete(cache_key)

    return {
        'statusCode': 200,
        'body': json.dumps({'message': 'Cache invalidated'})
    }

# Triggering invalidation
def update_user(user_id, new_data):
    # Update user in database
    # ...

    # Publish event
    sns.publish(
        TopicArn='arn:aws:sns:us-east-1:123456789012:UserUpdates',
        Message=json.dumps({'event_type': 'USER_UPDATE', 'user_id': user_id}),
    )
```

3. Read-Through Cache

The cache sits between the application and the data store. On a cache miss, the application fetches data from the store and updates the cache. This pattern is shown in the Lambda and Redis example above.

4. Write-Through Cache

In this pattern, all writes go through the cache and then to the database. This ensures that the cache is always updated, reducing the chance of stale data.

Implementing caching at both the edge and application layers significantly enhances the performance and scalability of serverless systems. Edge caching with CDNs like AWS CloudFront reduces latency and server load, while application layer caching with services like Redis (ElastiCache) minimizes database queries and speeds up response times. By adopting scalable architecture patterns such as microservices with isolated caches, event-driven cache invalidation, read-through caches, and write-through caches, serverless systems can handle increased load efficiently and provide a seamless user experience.

Invalidation Strategies: Keeping Caches Fresh and Consistent

In serverless architectures, caching is an essential strategy to improve performance and scalability. However, one of the significant challenges with caching is keeping the cached data fresh and consistent with the underlying data source. Effective cache invalidation strategies are crucial to ensuring that the cache remains an accurate reflection of the source data. This article explores various cache invalidation strategies, focusing on scalable software architecture patterns for serverless systems, along with code examples.

Overview of Cache Invalidation

Cache invalidation is the process of removing or updating stale data in the cache. This ensures that users receive up-to-date information without excessive latency from the backend. There are several strategies to handle cache invalidation:

1. Time-to-Live (TTL)

2. Event-Driven Invalidation

3. Write-Through and Write-Behind Caching

4. Read-Through Caching with Stale-While-Revalidate

Each of these strategies has its use cases, advantages, and trade-offs. We will delve into each strategy and provide code examples to illustrate how they can be implemented in a serverless environment.

1. Time-to-Live (TTL)

TTL is the simplest cache invalidation strategy, where each cache entry is given a lifespan. Once the TTL expires, the data is automatically removed from the cache.

Pros

- Simple to implement.
- Ensures data is eventually consistent.

Cons

- Stale data may be served until the TTL expires.
- Inefficient if data changes frequently.

Implementation Example with Redis and AWS Lambda

```python
import json
import redis
import os

redis_host = os.environ.get('REDIS_HOST')

def lambda_handler(event, context):
    r = redis.StrictRedis(host=redis_host, port 6379, db=0)

    cache_key = f"user:{event['user_id']}"
    user_data = r.get(cache_key)

    if user_data:
        return {
            'statusCode': 200,
            'body': json.dumps({'source': 'cache', 'data': json.loads(user_data)})
        }

    # Fetch from database (simulated)
    user_data = fetch_user_from_db(event['user_id'])

    # Cache the data with TTL
    r.setex(cache_key, 3600, json.dumps(user_data))
```

```
    return {
        'statusCode': 200,
        'body': json.dumps({'source': 'database', 'data': user_data})
    }

def fetch_user_from_db(user_id):
    # Simulate database fetch
    return {
        'user_id': user_id,
        'name': 'John Doe',
        'email': 'john.doe@example.com'
    }
```

2. Event-Driven Invalidation

In an event-driven invalidation strategy, cache invalidation occurs in response to specific events, such as data updates, deletions, or creation events. This approach ensures that the cache is updated as soon as the underlying data changes.

Pros

- High consistency between cache and source data.
- Efficient for frequently changing data.

Cons

- More complex to implement.

- Requires event handling infrastructure.

Implementation Example with AWS Lambda, SNS, and Redis

Step 1: Event Publisher

```python
import boto3
import json

sns = boto3.client('sns')

def update_user(user_id, new_data):
    # Update user in database
    # ...

    # Publish event to SNS
    sns.publish(
        TopicArn='arn:aws:sns:us-east-1:123456789012:UserUpdates',
        Message=json.dumps({'event_type': 'USER_UPDATE', 'user_id': user_id}),
```

)
```

## Step 2: Event Consumer

```python
import json
import redis
import os

redis_host = os.environ.get('REDIS_HOST')

def lambda_handler(event, context):
    r = redis.StrictRedis(host=redis_host, port 6379, db=0)

    # Invalidate cache upon receiving the event
    for record in event['Records']:
        message = json.loads(record['Sns']['Message'])
        if message['event_type'] == 'USER_UPDATE':
            cache_key = f"user:{message['user_id']}"
            r.delete(cache_key)

    return {
        'statusCode': 200,
        'body': json.dumps({'message': 'Cache invalidated'})
    }
```
```

3. Write-Through and Write-Behind Caching

Write-Through Caching: In this strategy, data is written to both the cache and the database simultaneously. This ensures that the cache is always up-to-date.

Pros

- Cache is always consistent with the database.
- Simple to implement.

Cons

- Slower writes due to dual writes.

Write-Behind Caching: Data is first written to the cache and then asynchronously written to the database. This improves write performance but may lead to inconsistency if the write to the database fails.

Pros

- Faster writes.
- Reduced latency for write operations.

Cons

- Potential for data inconsistency.

- Requires a robust mechanism to handle write failures.

Implementation Example with AWS Lambda and Redis (Write-Through)

```python
import json
import redis
import os

redis_host = os.environ.get('REDIS_HOST')

def lambda_handler(event, context):
    r = redis.StrictRedis(host=redis_host, port=6379, db=0)

    cache_key = f"user:{event['user_id']}"
    user_data = event['user_data']

    # Write to both cache and database
    r.set(cache_key, json.dumps(user_data))
    write_to_db(event['user_id'], user_data)
```

```
    return {
        'statusCode': 200,
        'body': json.dumps({'message': 'Data written to
cache and database'})
    }

def write_to_db(user_id, user_data):
    # Simulate database write
    pass
```
```

## 4. Read-Through Caching with Stale-While-Revalidate

In this strategy, data is read from the cache if available. If the data is stale, the stale data is served while a background process fetches and updates the cache with fresh data. This ensures that users receive data quickly while the cache is updated asynchronously.

### Pros

- Reduced latency for read operations.

- Ensures cache is eventually consistent.

### Cons
```

- Requires additional logic for background updates.

- Potentially stale data may be served temporarily.

Implementation Example with AWS Lambda and Redis

```python
import json
import redis
import os
import threading

redis_host = os.environ.get('REDIS_HOST')

def lambda_handler(event, context):
    r = redis.StrictRedis(host=redis_host, port=6379, db=0)

    cache_key = f"user:{event['user_id']}"
    user_data = r.get(cache_key)

    if user_data:
        # Spawn a background thread to update the cache
        threading.Thread(target=update_cache, args=(event['user_id'],)).start()
```

```python
    return {
        'statusCode': 200,
        'body': json.dumps({'source': 'cache', 'data': json.loads(user_data)})
    }

# Cache miss, fetch from database
user_data = fetch_user_from_db(event['user_id'])
r.set(cache_key, json.dumps(user_data))

return {
    'statusCode': 200,
    'body': json.dumps({'source': 'database', 'data': user_data})
}

def update_cache(user_id):
    r = redis.StrictRedis(host=redis_host, port 6379, db=0)
    cache_key = f"user:{user_id}"
    user_data = fetch_user_from_db(user_id)
    r.set(cache_key, json.dumps(user_data))

def fetch_user_from_db(user_id):
    # Simulate database fetch
    return {
        'user_id': user_id,
        'name': 'John Doe',
```

```
    'email': 'john.doe@example.com'
  }
```
```

Keeping caches fresh and consistent is crucial for the performance and reliability of serverless systems. Various strategies can be employed depending on the use case:

1. **Time-to-Live (TTL)**: Simple and effective for data that does not change frequently.

2. **Event-Driven Invalidation:** Ensures high consistency and is suitable for systems with frequent data changes.

3. **Write-Through and Write-Behind Caching:** Provides consistent cache states with trade-offs in write performance.

4. **Read-Through Caching with Stale-While-Revalidate:** Balances latency and data freshness by serving stale data temporarily while asynchronously updating the cache.

By understanding and implementing these strategies, serverless applications can maintain high performance and data accuracy, providing a seamless user experience.
```

Chapter 8

Asynchronous Workflows and Queues: Handling Long-Running Processes

Leveraging Queues for Asynchronous Processing: Offloading Work for Scalability

As serverless architectures become more prevalent, the need for efficient, scalable, and resilient processing models grows. One effective approach to achieve this is by leveraging queues for asynchronous processing. Queues enable applications to offload and decouple tasks, improving scalability and fault tolerance. This article explores how to implement asynchronous processing using queues in serverless systems, focusing on scalable software architecture patterns and providing code examples.

Benefits of Asynchronous Processing with Queues

1. Scalability: Queues help handle varying loads by decoupling components, allowing each to scale independently.

2. Fault Tolerance: If a task fails, it can be retried without affecting other parts of the system.

3. Performance: Offloading long-running or resource-intensive tasks to background processing can improve the responsiveness of the primary application.

4. Decoupling: Queues allow different parts of an application to be developed, deployed, and scaled independently.

Core Concepts

1. Message Queues: Queues like AWS SQS (Simple Queue Service) or Azure Queue Storage hold tasks or messages that need to be processed.

2. Producers: Components that send messages to the queue.

3. Consumers: Components that retrieve and process messages from the queue.

4. Dead-Letter Queues (DLQ): Special queues for handling messages that failed processing multiple times.

Architecture Patterns

1. Fan-Out Pattern: A single message is sent to multiple queues or services for parallel processing.

2. Chained Processing: Sequential processing where the output of one queue is the input for another.

3. Event-Driven Processing: Actions are triggered based on specific events, using queues to manage and process the events asynchronously.

Implementing Asynchronous Processing in Serverless Systems

Let's explore the implementation of these concepts using AWS Lambda and AWS SQS.

Setting Up AWS SQS

Step 1: Create an SQS Queue

```python
import boto3

sqs = boto3.client('sqs')

response = sqs.create_queue(
    QueueName='MyQueue',
    Attributes={
        'DelaySeconds': '0',
        'MessageRetentionPeriod': '86400'
    }
```

```
queue_url = response['QueueUrl']
print("Queue URL:", queue_url)
```

Producer: Sending Messages to the Queue

Step 2: Lambda Function to Send Messages

```python
import json
import boto3

sqs = boto3.client('sqs')
queue_url = 'https://sqs.us-east-1.amazonaws.com/123456789012/MyQueue'

def lambda_handler(event, context):
    message = {
        'user_id': event['user_id'],
        'action': 'process_data',
        'timestamp': event['timestamp']
    }

    response = sqs.send_message(
        QueueUrl=queue_url,
        MessageBody=json.dumps(message)
    )
```

```
    return {
        'statusCode': 200,
        'body': json.dumps({
            'message': 'Message sent to the queue',
            'messageId': response['MessageId']
        })
```
```

**Consumer: Processing Messages from the Queue**

**Step 3: Lambda Function to Process Messages**

```python
import json
import boto3

sqs = boto3.client('sqs')
queue_url = 'https://sqs.us-east-1.amazonaws.com/123456789012/MyQueue'

def lambda_handler(event, context):
    for record in event['Records']:
        message = json.loads(record['body'])
        process_message(message)

    return {
        'statusCode': 200,
```
```

```
        'body': json.dumps('Messages processed
successfully')
    }

def process_message(message):
    # Simulate processing
    print(f"Processing message: {message}")
```

Step 4: Trigger Lambda from SQS

Configure the SQS queue as an event source for the Lambda function. This can be done via the AWS Management Console, AWS CLI, or through infrastructure-as-code tools like AWS CloudFormation or Terraform.

```yaml
Resources:
  MyQueue:
    Type: AWS::SQS::Queue
    Properties:
      QueueName: MyQueue

  MyLambdaFunction:
    Type: AWS::Lambda::Function
    Properties:
      Handler: index.lambda_handler
```

```
      Runtime: python3.8
      Role: arn:aws:iam::123456789012:role/lambda-role
      Environment:
        Variables:
          QUEUE_URL: !Ref MyQueue

  MyLambdaQueueTrigger:
    Type: AWS::Lambda::EventSourceMapping
    Properties:
      BatchSize: 10
      EventSourceArn: !GetAtt MyQueue.Arn
      FunctionName: !GetAtt MyLambdaFunction.Arn
      Enabled: true
```

Advanced Patterns

1. Fan-Out Pattern

The Fan-Out pattern allows a single event to trigger multiple processing paths. This can be achieved using AWS SNS (Simple Notification Service) in combination with SQS.

Step 1: Create an SNS Topic

```python
import boto3
```

```python
sns = boto3.client('sns')

response = sns.create_topic(Name='MyTopic')
topic_arn = response['TopicArn']
print("Topic ARN:", topic_arn)
```

Step 2: Subscribe SQS Queues to the SNS Topic

```python
response = sns.subscribe(
    TopicArn=topic_arn,
    Protocol='sqs',
    Endpoint='https://sqs.us-east-1.amazonaws.com/123456789012/MyQueue'
)

response = sns.subscribe(
    TopicArn=topic_arn,
    Protocol='sqs',
    Endpoint='https://sqs.us-east-1.amazonaws.com/123456789012/AnotherQueue'
)
```

Step 3: Publish Messages to the SNS Topic

```python
def lambda_handler(event, context):
    message = {
        'user_id': event['user_id'],
        'action': 'process_data',
        'timestamp': event['timestamp']
    }

    response = sns.publish(
        TopicArn=topic_arn,
        Message=json.dumps(message)
    )

    return {
        'statusCode': 200,
        'body': json.dumps({
            'message': 'Message published to SNS topic',
            'messageId': response['MessageId']
        })
```

2. Chained Processing

Chained processing involves sequential tasks where the output of one process becomes the input for another. This can be achieved by using multiple SQS queues in sequence.

Step 1: Define Multiple Queues

```python
response = sqs.create_queue(QueueName='Queue1')
queue1_url = response['QueueUrl']

response = sqs.create_queue(QueueName='Queue2')
queue2_url = response['QueueUrl']
```

Step 2: Process Messages from Queue1 and Send to Queue2

```python
def lambda_handler(event, context):
    for record in event['Records']:
        message = json.loads(record['body'])
        processed_data = process_stage1(message)

        response = sqs.send_message(
            QueueUrl=queue2_url,
            MessageBody=json.dumps(processed_data)
        )

    return {
        'statusCode': 200,
        'body': json.dumps('Stage 1 processing complete')
    }
```

```python
def process_stage1(message):
    # Perform processing for stage 1
    message['stage1_processed'] = True
    return message
```

Step 3: Final Processing from Queue2

```python
def lambda_handler(event, context):
    for record in event['Records']:
        message = json.loads(record['body'])
        process_stage2(message)

    return {
        'statusCode': 200,
        'body': json.dumps('Stage 2 processing complete')
    }

def process_stage2(message):
    # Perform processing for stage 2
    print(f"Final processing of message: {message}")
```

Error Handling and Dead-Letter Queues

To ensure robustness, messages that fail processing should be sent to a Dead-Letter Queue (DLQ). This allows for monitoring and manual intervention if needed.

Step 1: Create a DLQ

```python
response = sqs.create_queue(QueueName='DLQ')
dlq_url = response['QueueUrl']
```

Step 2: Configure DLQ for the Main Queue

```yaml
Resources:
  MyQueue:
    Type: AWS::SQS::Queue
    Properties:
      QueueName: MyQueue
      RedrivePolicy:
        deadLetterTargetArn: !GetAtt MyDLQ.Arn
        maxReceiveCount: 5

  MyDLQ:
    Type: AWS::SQS::Queue
    Properties:
      QueueName: DLQ
```

Step 3: Handle Failed Messages

Messages that exceed the `maxReceiveCount` are automatically moved to the DLQ for further analysis.

```python
def lambda_handler(event, context):
    for record in event['Records']:
        try:
            message = json.loads(record['body'])
            process_message(message)
        except Exception as e:
            print(f"Error processing message: {e}")
            # Message will be retried or moved to DLQ after retries

    return {
        'statusCode': 200,
        'body': json.dumps('Processing complete')
    }

def process_message(message):
    # Simulate potential error
    if 'error' in message:
        raise ValueError("Simulated error")
    print(f"Processing message: {message}")
```

Leveraging queues for asynchronous processing in serverless architectures provides numerous benefits, including improved scalability, fault tolerance, and decoupling of components. By implementing scalable software architecture patterns such as Fan-Out, Chained Processing, and Event-Driven Processing, serverless applications can handle varying loads efficiently and maintain high performance.

Leveraging queues for asynchronous processing in serverless architectures provides numerous benefits, including improved scalability, fault tolerance, and decoupling of components. By implementing scalable software architecture patterns such as Fan-Out, Chained Processing, and Event-Driven Processing, serverless applications can handle varying loads efficiently and maintain high performance.

Example Use Case: Image Processing Pipeline

To illustrate the practical application of these concepts, let's consider an example of an image processing pipeline. In this scenario, users upload images that need to be processed (e.g., resized, filtered, and analyzed) asynchronously.

Architecture Overview

1. **Upload Service:** Receives images and stores them in S3.

2. **Resize Service**: Resizes images and stores the resized versions.

3. **Filter Service:** Applies filters to images.

4. **Analysis Service**: Analyzes images and extracts metadata.

5. **Notification Service:** Notifies users when processing is complete.

Each service communicates through SQS queues, allowing for scalable and decoupled processing.

Step 1: Upload Service (Producer)

When an image is uploaded, the Upload Service sends a message to the Resize Queue.

```python
import boto3
import json

s3 = boto3.client('s3')
```

```python
sqs = boto3.client('sqs')

resize_queue_url = 'https://sqs.us-east-1.amazonaws.com/123456789012/ResizeQueue'

def lambda_handler(event, context):
    for record in event['Records']:
        bucket = record['s3']['bucket']['name']
        key = record['s3']['object']['key']

        message = {
            'bucket': bucket,
            'key': key
        }

        sqs.send_message(
            QueueUrl=resize_queue_url,
            MessageBody=json.dumps(message)
        )

    return {
        'statusCode': 200,
        'body': json.dumps('Upload processed')
    }
```

Step 2: Resize Service (Consumer and Producer)

The Resize Service consumes messages from the Resize Queue, processes the images, and sends messages to the Filter Queue.

```python
import boto3
import json
from PIL import Image
from io import BytesIO

s3 = boto3.client('s3')
sqs = boto3.client('sqs')

filter_queue_url = 'https://sqs.us-east-1.amazonaws.com/123456789012/FilterQueue'

def lambda_handler(event, context):
    for record in event['Records']:
        message = json.loads(record['body'])
        bucket = message['bucket']
        key = message['key']

        image_data = s3.get_object(Bucket=bucket, Key=key)['Body'].read()
        image = Image.open(BytesIO(image_data))

        resized_image = image.resize((100, 100))  # Example resize operation
```

```
        resized_key = f"resized/{key}"
        out_buffer = BytesIO()
        resized_image.save(out_buffer,
format=image.format)
        out_buffer.seek(0)

        s3.put_object(Bucket=bucket, Key=resized_key,
Body=out_buffer)

        new_message = {
            'bucket': bucket,
            'key': resized_key
        }

        sqs.send_message(
            QueueUrl=filter_queue_url,
            MessageBody=json.dumps(new_message)
        )

    return {
        'statusCode': 200,
        'body': json.dumps('Resize processing complete')
    }
```

Step 3: Filter Service (Consumer and Producer)

The Filter Service consumes messages from the Filter Queue, applies filters, and sends messages to the Analysis Queue.

```python
import boto3
import json
from PIL import Image, ImageFilter
from io import BytesIO

s3 = boto3.client('s3')
sqs = boto3.client('sqs')

analysis_queue_url = 'https://sqs.us-east-1.amazonaws.com/123456789012/AnalysisQueue'

def lambda_handler(event, context):
    for record in event['Records']:
        message = json.loads(record['body'])
        bucket = message['bucket']
        key = message['key']

        image_data = s3.get_object(Bucket=bucket, Key=key)['Body'].read()
        image = Image.open(BytesIO(image_data))
```

```
        filtered_image =
image.filter(ImageFilter.CONTOUR)  # Example filter
operation

        filtered_key = f"filtered/{key}"
        out_buffer = BytesIO()
        filtered_image.save(out_buffer,
format=image.format)
        out_buffer.seek(0)

        s3.put_object(Bucket=bucket, Key=filtered_key,
Body=out_buffer)

        new_message = {
            'bucket': bucket,
            'key': filtered_key
        }

        sqs.send_message(
            QueueUrl=analysis_queue_url,
            MessageBody=json.dumps(new_message)
        )

    return {
        'statusCode': 200,
        'body': json.dumps('Filter processing complete')
    }
```

Step 4: Analysis Service (Consumer and Producer)

The Analysis Service consumes messages from the Analysis Queue, analyzes the images, and sends messages to the Notification Queue.

```python
import boto3
import json

s3 = boto3.client('s3')
sqs = boto3.client('sqs')

notification_queue_url = 'https://sqs.us-east-1.amazonaws.com/123456789012/NotificationQueue'

def lambda_handler(event, context):
    for record in event['Records']:
        message = json.loads(record['body'])
        bucket = message['bucket']
        key = message['key']

        # Example analysis: extract image metadata
        image_data = s3.get_object(Bucket=bucket, Key=key)['Body'].read()
        image = Image.open(BytesIO(image_data))
        metadata = {
```

```
        'format': image.format,
        'mode': image.mode,
        'size': image.size
    }

    new_message = {
        'bucket': bucket,
        'key': key,
        'metadata': metadata
    }

    sqs.send_message(
        QueueUrl=notification_queue_url,
        MessageBody=json.dumps(new_message)
    )

    return {
        'statusCode': 200,
        'body': json.dumps('Analysis processing complete')
    }
```

Step 5: Notification Service (Consumer)

The Notification Service consumes messages from the Notification Queue and sends a notification to the user.

```python
```

```python
import boto3
import json

sns = boto3.client('sns')

def lambda_handler(event, context):
    for record in event['Records']:
        message = json.loads(record['body'])
        bucket = message['bucket']
        key = message['key']
        metadata = message['metadata']

        notification_message = f"Image {key} processed with metadata: {metadata}"

        sns.publish(
            TopicArn='arn:aws:sns:us-east-1:123456789012:UserNotifications',
            Message=notification_message
        )

    return {
        'statusCode': 200,
        'body': json.dumps('Notification sent')
    }
```

Asynchronous processing using queues is a powerful technique for building scalable and resilient serverless applications. By decoupling components and offloading tasks, we can handle varying loads more efficiently and ensure that the system remains responsive and fault-tolerant.

By leveraging different patterns such as Fan-Out, Chained Processing, and Event-Driven Processing, we can design complex workflows that are both maintainable and scalable. Additionally, incorporating error handling mechanisms such as Dead-Letter Queues ensures robustness and helps in managing failures gracefully.

These patterns and implementations form the backbone of modern serverless architectures, allowing developers to build highly performant and scalable applications that can handle diverse and demanding workloads.

Choosing the Right Queueing System for Your Needs: Managed vs. Self-Hosted

Asynchronous processing with queueing systems is essential for building scalable, resilient, and decoupled serverless applications. Choosing the right queueing system can significantly impact the overall performance, cost, and maintainability of your architecture. This article will explore the differences between managed and self-hosted queueing systems, providing guidance on how to select the best option for your specific needs and offering code examples to illustrate the concepts.

Managed vs. Self-Hosted Queueing Systems

Managed Queueing Systems

Managed queueing systems are fully hosted and maintained by cloud providers. Examples include AWS SQS, Azure Queue Storage, and Google Cloud Pub/Sub. These services offer built-in scalability, high availability, and integration with other cloud services. They are ideal for organizations that prefer to offload infrastructure management to a third party.

Advantages of Managed Queueing Systems:

1. Scalability: Automatically scales to handle varying loads without manual intervention.

2. High Availability: Built-in redundancy and failover mechanisms ensure high uptime.

3. Ease of Use: Simplifies setup and management with user-friendly interfaces and integrations.

4. Cost Efficiency: Pay-as-you-go pricing models reduce the need for upfront investment in hardware.

Disadvantages of Managed Queueing Systems:

1. Vendor Lock-In: Tightly coupled with specific cloud providers, making it harder to migrate to other platforms.

2. Limited Customization: Less control over underlying infrastructure and configurations.

Self-Hosted Queueing Systems

Self-hosted queueing systems require you to manage and maintain the infrastructure. Examples include RabbitMQ, Apache Kafka, and ActiveMQ. These systems provide greater control and customization but require more effort to deploy, scale, and maintain.

Advantages of Self-Hosted Queueing Systems:

1. Customization: Full control over configurations, allowing for tailored optimizations.

2. Flexibility: Can be deployed on any infrastructure, providing more options for hybrid or multi-cloud environments.

3. No Vendor Lock-In: Easier to migrate between different hosting environments or providers.

Disadvantages of Self-Hosted Queueing Systems:

1. Complexity: Requires significant expertise to set up, configure, and manage.

2. Maintenance: Ongoing responsibility for updates, scaling, and troubleshooting.

3. Cost: Higher upfront costs for hardware and potentially higher operational costs.

Criteria for Choosing Between Managed and Self-Hosted Queueing Systems

1. Scalability Requirements

- Managed: If you anticipate unpredictable or highly variable workloads, a managed system can automatically scale to meet demand without manual intervention.

- **Self-Hosted:** Suitable for more predictable workloads where you can plan and manage scaling.

2. Control and Customization

- **Managed**: If you need rapid deployment with minimal configuration, managed systems are ideal.

- **Self-Hosted:** If your application requires specific configurations or custom optimizations, a self-hosted system provides the necessary flexibility.

3. Integration and Ecosystem

- **Managed**: If you are already heavily invested in a specific cloud provider's ecosystem (e.g., AWS, Azure, Google Cloud), using their managed queueing services can simplify integration and management.

- **Self-Hosted:** If you need a multi-cloud or hybrid-cloud approach, a self-hosted solution can be more adaptable.

4. Cost Considerations

- **Managed**: Pay-as-you-go models can be cost-effective for variable workloads, reducing upfront costs.

- **Self-Hosted:** For large-scale, predictable workloads, self-hosted solutions can sometimes be more economical in the long run, despite higher initial costs.

Implementing Queueing Systems in Serverless Architectures

Example 1: Using AWS SQS (Managed)

AWS SQS is a managed queueing service that integrates seamlessly with other AWS services, making it an excellent choice for serverless architectures.

Step 1: Create an SQS Queue

```python
import boto3

sqs = boto3.client('sqs')

response = sqs.create_queue(
    QueueName='MyQueue',
    Attributes={
        'DelaySeconds': '0',
        'MessageRetentionPeriod': '86400'
    }
```

```
queue_url = response['QueueUrl']
print("Queue URL:", queue_url)
```

Step 2: Send Messages to the Queue

```python
import boto3
import json

sqs = boto3.client('sqs')
queue_url = 'https://sqs.us-east-1.amazonaws.com/123456789012/MyQueue'

def lambda_handler(event, context):
    message = {
        'user_id': event['user_id'],
        'action': 'process_data',
        'timestamp': event['timestamp']
    }

    response = sqs.send_message(
        QueueUrl=queue_url,
        MessageBody=json.dumps(message)
    )

    return {
        'statusCode': 200,
```

```
    'body': json.dumps({
        'message': 'Message sent to the queue',
        'messageId': response['MessageId']
    })
```

Step 3: Process Messages from the Queue

```python
import boto3
import json

sqs = boto3.client('sqs')
queue_url = 'https://sqs.us-east-1.amazonaws.com/123456789012/MyQueue'

def lambda_handler(event, context):
    for record in event['Records']:
        message = json.loads(record['body'])
        process_message(message)

    return {
        'statusCode': 200,
        'body': json.dumps('Messages processed successfully')
    }
```

```
def process_message(message):
    # Simulate processing
    print(f"Processing message: {message}")
```

Example 2: Using RabbitMQ (Self-Hosted)

RabbitMQ is a widely-used open-source message broker that can be self-hosted on various infrastructures.

Step 1: Set Up RabbitMQ Server

Install RabbitMQ on your server. For instance, on an Ubuntu server, you can use:

```bash
sudo apt-get update
sudo apt-get install -y rabbitmq-server
sudo systemctl enable rabbitmq-server
sudo systemctl start rabbitmq-server
```

Step 2: Send Messages to RabbitMQ

```python
import pika
import json
```

```python
def send_message(message):
    connection = pika.BlockingConnection(pika.ConnectionParameters('localhost'))
    channel = connection.channel()

    channel.queue_declare(queue='my_queue')

    channel.basic_publish(exchange='', routing_key='my_queue', body=json.dumps(message))
    print("Sent:", message)

    connection.close()

# Example usage
send_message({'user_id': 123, 'action': 'process_data', 'timestamp': '2024-05-24T12:00:00Z'})
```

Step 3: Consume Messages from RabbitMQ

```python
import pika
import json

def process_message(ch, method, properties, body):
    message = json.loads(body)
    print("Received:", message)
```

```
    # Simulate processing
    ch.basic_ack(delivery_tag=method.delivery_tag)

connection = pika.BlockingConnection(pika.ConnectionParameters('localhost'))
channel = connection.channel()

channel.queue_declare(queue='my_queue')

channel.basic_consume(queue='my_queue', on_message_callback=process_message)

print('Waiting for messages...')
channel.start_consuming()
```

Best Practices and Considerations

1. Security: Ensure that your queueing system is secure. For managed services, leverage IAM roles and policies. For self-hosted systems, configure proper network security and access controls.

2. Monitoring and Logging: Implement robust monitoring and logging to track message flow and detect issues early. Managed services often provide built-in monitoring tools. For self-hosted systems, tools like Prometheus and Grafana can be integrated.

3. Error Handling: Use Dead-Letter Queues (DLQ) to handle failed messages gracefully. Both managed and self-hosted systems support DLQs, although implementation details vary.

4. Scalability Testing: Regularly test the scalability of your queueing system under expected and peak loads to ensure it can handle real-world traffic.

Choosing the right queueing system for your serverless architecture involves evaluating your specific needs, including scalability, control, integration, and cost. Managed queueing systems like AWS SQS offer ease of use, automatic scaling, and seamless integration with other cloud services, making them ideal for many serverless applications. Self-hosted solutions like RabbitMQ provide greater control and customization, which can be beneficial for specialized requirements or hybrid environments.

By carefully considering these factors and following best practices, you can implement a robust, scalable, and efficient queueing system that supports your serverless application's asynchronous processing needs.

Implementing Retries and Dead-Lettering for Robustness in Serverless Systems

In serverless architectures, ensuring the robustness of asynchronous processing is crucial for maintaining reliability and resilience. Implementing retries and dead-letter queues (DLQs) are essential techniques to handle transient failures and ensure that unprocessed messages are not lost. This article delves into the principles, patterns, and best practices for implementing retries and dead-lettering in serverless systems, with code examples to illustrate the concepts.

Importance of Retries and Dead-Lettering

Retries

Retries are mechanisms to automatically reprocess failed operations. They help in mitigating transient issues such as network glitches, temporary unavailability of services, or momentary overloads. By retrying failed operations, systems can often recover without manual intervention, improving overall reliability and user experience.

Dead-Letter Queues (DLQs)

DLQs are specialized queues that store messages that cannot be successfully processed after a defined number of retries. This ensures that problematic messages are not lost but can be reviewed and handled separately, preventing them from blocking or overloading the main processing workflow.

Patterns and Best Practices

1. Idempotent Operations: Ensure that operations are idempotent, meaning that retrying an operation multiple times has the same effect as executing it once. This avoids issues such as duplicate entries or inconsistent states.

2. Exponential Backoff: Use exponential backoff strategies for retries to prevent overwhelming the system and to allow time for transient issues to resolve.

3. Separate Concerns: Decouple the retry logic from the main processing logic to maintain clarity and manageability of the code.

4. Monitoring and Alerting: Implement robust monitoring and alerting for DLQs to ensure that failed messages are addressed promptly.

Implementing Retries and DLQs with AWS SQS and Lambda

AWS SQS (Simple Queue Service) and Lambda are popular choices for building serverless applications that require asynchronous processing. Below, we demonstrate how to implement retries and DLQs using these services.

Step 1: Create the Main Queue and DLQ

First, create an SQS queue for the main processing and another queue for dead-lettering.

```python
import boto3

sqs = boto3.client('sqs')

# Create Dead-Letter Queue
dlq_response = sqs.create_queue(
    QueueName='MyDLQ',
    Attributes={
        'MessageRetentionPeriod': '86400'  # 1 day
    }
)

dlq_url = dlq_response['QueueUrl']

# Get the ARN of the DLQ
dlq_arn = sqs.get_queue_attributes(
    QueueUrl=dlq_url,
    AttributeNames=['QueueArn']
)['Attributes']['QueueArn']

# Create Main Queue with DLQ configuration
main_queue_response = sqs.create_queue(
```

```
        QueueName='MyMainQueue',
        Attributes={
            'DelaySeconds': '0',
            'MessageRetentionPeriod': '86400',
            'RedrivePolicy': json.dumps({
                'deadLetterTargetArn': dlq_arn,
                'maxReceiveCount': '5'  # Number of retries
            })
main_queue_url = main_queue_response['QueueUrl']
print("Main Queue URL:", main_queue_url)
print("DLQ URL:", dlq_url)
```

Step 2: Lambda Function to Process Messages

Create a Lambda function to process messages from the main queue. This function includes retry logic.

```python
import boto3
import json
```

```
import time

sqs = boto3.client('sqs')

def lambda_handler(event, context):
    for record in event['Records']:
        try:
            message = json.loads(record['body'])
            process_message(message)
        except Exception as e:
            print(f"Error processing message: {e}")
            raise e  # Raising the exception to trigger retry

def process_message(message):
    # Simulate processing and potential failure
    if message.get('fail', False):
        raise Exception("Simulated processing failure")
    print(f"Processed message: {message}")
```
```

**Step 3: Configure Lambda Event Source Mapping**
```

Configure the Lambda function to trigger on messages from the main SQS queue.

```python
import boto3

lambda_client = boto3.client('lambda')

response = lambda_client.create_event_source_mapping(
    EventSourceArn=main_queue_arn,
    FunctionName='MyLambdaFunction',
    Enabled=True,
    BatchSize=10,
    MaximumBatchingWindowInSeconds=60
)

print("Event Source Mapping ARN:", response['UUID'])
```

Implementing Retries and DLQs with RabbitMQ

For those who prefer self-hosted solutions, RabbitMQ is a popular choice. Here's how to implement retries and DLQs with RabbitMQ.

Step 1: Setup RabbitMQ

First, ensure RabbitMQ is installed and running on your server. You can use Docker for a quick setup.

```bash
docker run -d --name rabbitmq -p 5672:5672 -p 15672:15672 rabbitmq:3-management
```

Step 2: Define Queues and Exchanges

Define the main queue, DLQ, and exchanges in RabbitMQ.

```python
import pika
import json

# Establish connection and channel
connection = pika.BlockingConnection(pika.ConnectionParameters('localhost'))
channel = connection.channel()

# Declare DLQ
channel.queue_declare(queue='dlq', durable=True)
```

```python
# Declare main queue with DLQ configuration
args = {
    'x-dead-letter-exchange': '',
    'x-dead-letter-routing-key': 'dlq',
    'x-message-ttl': 60000  # TTL for messages in milliseconds
}
channel.queue_declare(queue='main_queue', durable=True, arguments=args)

# Declare exchange
channel.exchange_declare(exchange='main_exchange', exchange_type='direct')

# Bind queue to exchange
channel.queue_bind(exchange='main_exchange', queue='main_queue', routing_key='main_key')

connection.close()
```

Step 3: Publish Messages to the Queue

Publish messages to the main queue.

```python
import pika
import json

def send_message(message):
    connection = pika.BlockingConnection(pika.ConnectionParameters('localhost'))
    channel = connection.channel()
    channel.basic_publish(
        exchange='main_exchange',
        routing_key='main_key',
        body=json.dumps(message),
        properties=pika.BasicProperties(
            delivery_mode=2,  # Make message persistent
        )
    )
    print("Sent:", message)
    connection.close()

# Example usage
```

```
send_message({'user_id': 123, 'action': 'process_data', 'fail': True})
```

Step 4: Consume Messages with Retry Logic

Consume messages from the main queue with retry logic.

```python
import pika
import json
import time

def process_message(ch, method, properties, body):
    message = json.loads(body)
    try:
        if message.get('fail', False):
            raise Exception("Simulated processing failure")
        print(f"Processed message: {message}")
        ch.basic_ack(delivery_tag=method.delivery_tag)
    except Exception as e:
```

```
        print(f"Error processing message: {e}")

        ch.basic_nack(delivery_tag=method.delivery_tag, requeue=False)  # Move to DLQ

connection = pika.BlockingConnection(pika.ConnectionParameters('localhost'))

channel = connection.channel()

channel.basic_qos(prefetch_count=1)

channel.basic_consume(queue='main_queue', on_message_callback=process_message)

print('Waiting for messages...')

channel.start_consuming()
```

Monitoring and Handling DLQs

Monitoring DLQs is essential to ensure that failed messages are addressed. This can be achieved through cloud provider dashboards or custom monitoring solutions.

AWS CloudWatch for SQS

For AWS SQS, CloudWatch can be used to monitor DLQs.

```python
import boto3
cloudwatch = boto3.client('cloudwatch')
response = cloudwatch.get_metric_statistics(
    Namespace='AWS/SQS',
    MetricName='ApproximateNumberOfMessagesVisible',
    Dimensions=[
        {'Name': 'QueueName', 'Value': 'MyDLQ'}
    ],
    StartTime=datetime.utcnow() - timedelta(hours=1),
    EndTime=datetime.utcnow(),
    Period=300,
    Statistics=['Average']
)
print("DLQ message count:", response['Datapoints'])
```

RabbitMQ Management Plugin

For RabbitMQ, the management plugin provides a UI for monitoring queues, including DLQs.

```bash
# Enable RabbitMQ management plugin
docker exec rabbitmq rabbitmq-plugins enable rabbitmq_management
```

Implementing retries and dead-letter queues is crucial for building robust and resilient serverless applications. Retries help mitigate transient issues, while DLQs ensure that problematic messages are not lost but can be reviewed and handled separately. By following best practices such as ensuring idempotent operations, using exponential backoff strategies, and implementing robust monitoring and alerting, you can significantly improve the reliability and resilience of your serverless architecture.

Both managed services like AWS SQS and self-hosted solutions like RabbitMQ provide robust mechanisms for retries and dead-lettering, allowing you to choose the best fit for your specific requirements. With careful planning and implementation, you can build scalable, resilient, and maintainable serverless systems that handle failures gracefully.

Chapter 9

Scaling for High Traffic: Techniques for Handling Peak Loads

Identifying Scaling Triggers: Monitoring Metrics for Proactive Scalability

Scaling is a fundamental aspect of building robust and resilient software systems, particularly in serverless environments where resources are provisioned on-demand. The ability to scale effectively can mean the difference between a performant application and one that buckles under load. To achieve proactive scalability, it is crucial to monitor the right metrics and understand the triggers that necessitate scaling. This article explores the key metrics to monitor and demonstrates how to implement scalable software architecture patterns for serverless systems using code examples.

Key Metrics for Monitoring Scalability

1. Invocation Count

The number of times a function is invoked is a primary metric for understanding the load on your serverless system. High invocation rates can indicate a need for scaling to handle increased traffic.

2. Execution Duration

Monitoring how long each function execution takes helps identify performance bottlenecks. Functions that consistently run for extended periods might need optimization or increased resource allocation.

3. Concurrency

Concurrency measures the number of functions running simultaneously. Exceeding the concurrency limit can lead to throttling. Monitoring this metric ensures you can preemptively scale resources to avoid performance degradation.

4. Error Rates

Error rates, including timeouts and failures, can indicate problems in your application that require scaling to manage fault tolerance or adjusting logic to handle increased loads.

5. Resource Utilization

Metrics like memory and CPU usage provide insight into how efficiently your functions are operating. High resource usage may require scaling to larger instance sizes or distributing the load across more instances.

Scalable Software Architecture Patterns

Event-Driven Architecture

Event-driven architecture is a common pattern in serverless applications. It involves building applications as a series of loosely coupled events that trigger serverless functions. This architecture naturally supports scalability, as each event can trigger a function that operates independently.

```python
import boto3

def lambda_handler(event, context):
    # Your function logic here
    print("Event received: ", event)

# Example event triggering in AWS Lambda
event = {
    'Records': [
        {
            'eventID': '1',
            'eventName': 'INSERT',
            'eventVersion': '1.0',
            'eventSource': 'aws:dynamodb',
            'awsRegion': 'us-east-1',
```

```
            'dynamodb': {
                'Keys': {
                    'Id': {
                        'N': '101'
                    }
                },
                'NewImage': {
                    'Message': {
                        'S': 'New item!'
                    }
                }
lambda_handler(event, None)
```

Microservices

Breaking down applications into microservices allows for each service to scale independently. This pattern is particularly effective in serverless environments where each microservice can be implemented as a separate function.

```python
# user_service.py
def create_user(event, context):
    # Logic to create a user
    pass
```

```python
# order_service.py
def create_order(event, context):
    # Logic to create an order
    pass

# product_service.py
def create_product(event, context):
    # Logic to create a product
    pass
```

Queue-Based Load Leveling

Queue-based load leveling involves using message queues to handle bursts of traffic by smoothing out the load over time. AWS SQS (Simple Queue Service) and Azure Queue Storage are common choices for implementing this pattern.

```python
import boto3

sqs = boto3.client('sqs')

def send_message_to_queue(message_body):
    response = sqs.send_message(
        QueueUrl='https://sqs.us-east-1.amazonaws.com/123456789012/MyQueue',
```

```
        MessageBody=message_body
    )
    print("Message sent with ID:", response['MessageId'])

def lambda_handler(event, context):
    # Logic to handle event and send to SQS
    send_message_to_queue('Hello, this is a test message!')
```

Implementing Proactive Scalability

Monitoring Metrics with CloudWatch

AWS CloudWatch provides a comprehensive suite of monitoring tools that allow you to keep an eye on key metrics and set alarms to trigger scaling actions.

```python
import boto3

cloudwatch = boto3.client('cloudwatch')

def create_alarm():
    cloudwatch.put_metric_alarm(
        AlarmName='HighInvocationRate',
        MetricName='Invocations',
        Namespace='AWS/Lambda',
```

```
        Statistic='Sum',
        Period=60,
        EvaluationPeriods=1,
        Threshold=100,
        ComparisonOperator='GreaterThanThreshold',
        Dimensions=[
            {
                'Name': 'FunctionName',
                'Value': 'my-lambda-function'
            }
        ],
        AlarmActions=[
            'arn:aws:autoscaling:us-east-1:123456789012:scalingPolicy:policy-id:autoScalingGroupName/group-name'
        ]

    print("Alarm created successfully.")

create_alarm()
```

Autoscaling with AWS Lambda

AWS Lambda automatically scales your applications by adjusting the number of concurrent executions based on the traffic. To enhance this, you can use Lambda Provisioned Concurrency to ensure a certain number of function instances are always ready to respond.

```python
import boto3

lambda_client = boto3.client('lambda')

def provisioned_concurrency(function_name, provisioned_concurrent_executions):
    response = lambda_client.put_provisioned_concurrency_config(
        FunctionName=function_name,
        Qualifier='$LATEST',
        ProvisionedConcurrentExecutions=provisioned_concurrent_executions
    )
    print("Provisioned concurrency set:", response)

provisioned_concurrency('my-lambda-function', 10)
```

Horizontal Pod Autoscaling in Kubernetes

For containerized serverless architectures using Kubernetes, Horizontal Pod Autoscaling (HPA) can be used to scale the number of pod replicas based on CPU utilization or custom metrics.

```yaml
apiVersion: autoscaling/v1
kind: HorizontalPodAutoscaler
metadata:
  name: my-app-hpa
spec:
  scaleTargetRef:
    apiVersion: apps/v1
    kind: Deployment
    name: my-app
  minReplicas: 1
  maxReplicas: 10
  targetCPUUtilizationPercentage: 50
```

Utilizing Serverless Frameworks

Serverless frameworks like Serverless Framework, AWS SAM (Serverless Application Model), and the Azure Functions framework can simplify the deployment and scaling of serverless applications by abstracting the infrastructure management.

```yaml
# serverless.yml
service: my-service

provider:
```

```
name: aws
runtime: python3.8

functions:
  hello:
    handler: handler.hello
    events:
      - http:
          path: hello
          method: get

resources:
  Resources:
    MyDynamoDBTable:
      Type: AWS::DynamoDB::Table
      Properties:
        TableName: MyTable
        AttributeDefinitions:
          - AttributeName: Id
            AttributeType: S
        KeySchema:
          - AttributeName: Id
            KeyType: HASH
        ProvisionedThroughput:
          ReadCapacityUnits: 1
          WriteCapacityUnits: 1
```

Monitoring the right metrics and understanding the triggers for scaling are crucial in building scalable serverless applications. Key metrics such as invocation count, execution duration, concurrency, error rates, and resource utilization provide insight into your application's performance and help you anticipate the need for scaling. Implementing scalable software architecture patterns like event-driven architecture, microservices, and queue-based load leveling ensures that your application can handle increased load effectively.

Proactive scalability can be achieved using tools like AWS CloudWatch for monitoring and AWS Lambda's provisioned concurrency for ensuring readiness. Kubernetes' Horizontal Pod Autoscaling can manage containerized workloads, and serverless frameworks streamline deployment and scaling processes. By adopting these strategies, you can build serverless systems that are resilient, efficient, and capable of handling dynamic workloads.

Auto-Scaling Techniques: Dynamically Adjusting Resources Based on Demand

In the realm of cloud computing, auto-scaling is a crucial feature that ensures applications can handle varying loads efficiently without manual intervention. Auto-scaling dynamically adjusts the allocation of resources based on demand, allowing applications to maintain performance and optimize costs. In serverless architectures, this capability is integral as it leverages the inherent flexibility and scalability of the cloud. This article explores various auto-scaling techniques, demonstrates their implementation through code examples, and discusses scalable software architecture patterns for serverless systems.

Key Auto-Scaling Techniques

1. Horizontal Scaling (Scaling Out/In)

2. Vertical Scaling (Scaling Up/Down)

3. Predictive Scaling

4. Scheduled Scaling

5. Reactive Scaling

1. Horizontal Scaling (Scaling Out/In)

Horizontal scaling involves adding or removing instances to handle changes in load. This technique is particularly useful for stateless applications where each instance can operate independently.

Example: AWS Lambda with DynamoDB Streams

In a serverless context, AWS Lambda can automatically scale out in response to events such as DynamoDB stream records.

```python
import boto3

dynamodb = boto3.resource('dynamodb')
table = dynamodb.Table('MyTable')

def lambda_handler(event, context):
    for record in event['Records']:
        if record['eventName'] == 'INSERT':
            new_item = record['dynamodb']['NewImage']
            print(f"New item added: {new_item}")
    return 'Processed {} records.'.format(len(event['Records']))
```

2. Vertical Scaling (Scaling Up/Down)

Vertical scaling involves changing the size of the instances (e.g., increasing CPU, memory) to handle an increased load. In serverless systems, this is less common because serverless functions abstract away the infrastructure details.

Example: AWS Lambda with Provisioned Concurrency

AWS Lambda can use Provisioned Concurrency to ensure a certain number of function instances are always ready to respond to increased load, effectively "scaling up" the available resources.

```python
import boto3

lambda_client = boto3.client('lambda')

def provisioned_concurrency(function_name, provisioned_concurrent_executions):
    response = lambda_client.put_provisioned_concurrency_config(
        FunctionName=function_name,
        Qualifier='$LATEST',
        ProvisionedConcurrentExecutions=provisioned_concurrent_executions
    )
    print("Provisioned concurrency set:", response)

provisioned_concurrency('my-lambda-function', 10)
```

3. Predictive Scaling

Predictive scaling uses machine learning to anticipate future load based on historical data and trends, adjusting resources accordingly before the demand actually hits.

Example: AWS Auto Scaling with Predictive Scaling Policy

AWS Auto Scaling offers predictive scaling policies to automatically adjust resources based on predicted future demand.

```yaml
Resources:
  MyAutoScalingGroup:
    Type: AWS::AutoScaling::AutoScalingGroup
    Properties:
      MinSize: 1
      MaxSize: 10
      DesiredCapacity: 2
      PredictiveScalingConfiguration:
        MetricSpecifications:
          - TargetValue: 50
            PredefinedScalingMetricSpecification:
              PredefinedScalingMetricType: ASGAverageCPUUtilization
```

        Mode: ForecastAndScale
```

## 4. Scheduled Scaling

Scheduled scaling adjusts resources based on a predefined schedule. This is useful for predictable workloads, such as processing batch jobs during off-peak hours.

### Example: AWS Lambda Scheduled Scaling with CloudWatch Events

You can use Amazon CloudWatch Events to trigger AWS Lambda functions based on a schedule.

```yaml
Resources:
  MyScheduledEvent:
    Type: AWS::Events::Rule
    Properties:
      ScheduleExpression: 'rate(1 hour)'
      Targets:
        - Arn: arn:aws:lambda:us-east-1:123456789012:function:my-lambda-function
          Id: "MyLambdaFunction"
```
```

5. Reactive Scaling

Reactive scaling responds to real-time changes in metrics such as CPU utilization, memory usage, or request rates. This ensures that the application can handle sudden spikes in demand.

Example: AWS Lambda Reactive Scaling with CloudWatch Alarms

Using CloudWatch Alarms, you can trigger scaling actions based on specific thresholds.

```python
import boto3

cloudwatch = boto3.client('cloudwatch')

def create_alarm():
    cloudwatch.put_metric_alarm(
        AlarmName='HighInvocationRate',
        MetricName='Invocations',
        Namespace='AWS/Lambda',
        Statistic='Sum',
        Period=60,
        EvaluationPeriods=1,
        Threshold=100,
        ComparisonOperator='GreaterThanThreshold',
```

```
        Dimensions=[
          {
            'Name': 'FunctionName',
            'Value': 'my-lambda-function'
          }

        AlarmActions=[
          'arn:aws:autoscaling:us-east-1:123456789012:scalingPolicy:policy-id:autoScalingGroupName/group-name'
        ]

        print("Alarm created successfully.")

create_alarm()
```

Scalable Software Architecture Patterns for Serverless Systems

Event-Driven Architecture

Event-driven architecture is ideal for serverless systems. It decouples the components of the system, allowing each to scale independently in response to events.

Example: AWS Lambda with S3 Events

```python
import boto3

s3 = boto3.client('s3')

def lambda_handler(event, context):
    for record in event['Records']:
        bucket = record['s3']['bucket']['name']
        key = record['s3']['object']['key']
        print(f"New file uploaded to {bucket}/{key}")

# S3 Event Configuration (not in code, done via S3 console or CloudFormation)
```

Microservices

Microservices architecture decomposes an application into smaller, loosely coupled services that can be developed, deployed, and scaled independently.

Example: AWS Lambda with API Gateway

```python
# user_service.py
def create_user(event, context):
    # Logic to create a user
    pass
```

```python
# order_service.py
def create_order(event, context):
    # Logic to create an order
    pass

# product_service.py
def create_product(event, context):
    # Logic to create a product
    pass
```

```yaml
# serverless.yml
service: my-microservices

provider:
  name: aws
  runtime: python3.8

functions:
  createUser:
    handler: user_service.create_user
    events:
      - http:
          path: user
          method: post
  createOrder:
    handler: order_service.create_order
    events:
```

```yaml
      - http:
          path: order
          method: post
  createProduct:
    handler: product_service.create_product
    events:
      - http:
          path: product
          method: post
```

Queue-Based Load Leveling

Queue-based load leveling uses message queues to manage the load by decoupling the request submission from request processing, effectively smoothing out bursts in traffic.

Example: AWS Lambda with SQS

```python
import boto3

sqs = boto3.client('sqs')

def send_message_to_queue(message_body):
    response = sqs.send_message(
```

```
        QueueUrl='https://sqs.us-east-
1.amazonaws.com/123456789012/MyQueue',
        MessageBody=message_body
    )
    print("Message sent with ID:", response['MessageId'])

def lambda_handler(event, context):
    # Logic to handle event and send to SQS
    send_message_to_queue('Hello, this is a test message!')
```
```

Auto-scaling is a cornerstone of building scalable and resilient serverless applications. Techniques like horizontal and vertical scaling, predictive scaling, scheduled scaling, and reactive scaling ensure that applications can dynamically adjust resources based on demand, maintaining performance and optimizing costs. By implementing scalable software architecture patterns such as event-driven architecture, microservices, and queue-based load leveling, developers can build robust serverless systems capable of handling varying workloads efficiently.

By leveraging tools and services like AWS Lambda, CloudWatch, SQS, and API Gateway, developers can create auto-scaling mechanisms that respond to real-time metrics and anticipated loads. These practices not only
```

enhance the application's ability to handle spikes in demand but also contribute to a more cost-effective and maintainable architecture. Embracing these auto-scaling techniques and patterns is essential for any modern serverless application aiming for high availability and performance.

Handling Cold Starts: Optimizing Function Startup Times

Cold starts are a well-known challenge in serverless computing, where the function execution environment is spun up on demand, often leading to latency that can degrade performance. This article delves into strategies for optimizing function startup times, supported by code examples and based on scalable software architecture patterns for serverless systems.

Understanding Cold Start

When a serverless function is invoked, the cloud provider initializes a new execution environment if there isn't a warm one available. This initialization involves several steps, including downloading the function code, initializing dependencies, and running any startup scripts. The time taken for these steps is referred to as the cold start latency. In contrast, a warm start occurs when an existing execution environment is reused, avoiding most of the initialization overhead.

Strategies to Optimize Cold Starts

1. Minimize Function Code Size

The size of the deployment package directly impacts cold start times. Smaller packages reduce the time required for downloading and initializing the function. This can be achieved through several practices:

- **Tree Shaking:** Remove dead code and unused dependencies.
- **Layering**: Use AWS Lambda Layers or similar features in other cloud providers to share common dependencies across functions.

```javascript
// Example of a minimal Node.js Lambda function

const aws = require('aws-sdk');

exports.handler = async (event) => {
  const s3 = new aws.S3();
  const params = {
    Bucket: 'example-bucket',
    Key: 'example-key'
  };
  const data = await s3.getObject(params).promise();
  return data.Body.toString();
```

};
```

## 2. Optimize Dependencies

Dependencies can significantly impact the initialization time. Optimize by reducing the number of dependencies and only including those that are necessary.

- **Selective Import:** Import only the necessary parts of a module.

```javascript
// Instead of importing the entire aws-sdk, import only the required service
const { S3 } = require('aws-sdk');

exports.handler = async (event) => {
  const s3 = new S3();
  const params = {
    Bucket: 'example-bucket',
    Key: 'example-key'
  };
  const data = await s3.getObject(params).promise();
```
```

```
    return data.Body.toString();
};
```

3. Warm Up Strategies

Keeping functions warm can prevent cold starts. There are several ways to achieve this:

- **Scheduled Invocations:** Use a scheduled task to periodically invoke functions, keeping them warm.

```yaml
# Example of AWS CloudFormation configuration for scheduled Lambda invocations

WarmUpFunction:
  Type: 'AWS::Lambda::Function'
  Properties:
    Handler: index.handler
    Runtime: nodejs14.x
    Timeout: 30
    MemorySize: 128
```

```
      Role: !GetAtt LambdaExecutionRole.Arn
      Code:
        ZipFile: |
          exports.handler = async (event) => {
            console.log("Warming up function");
          };
  WarmUpRule:
    Type: 'AWS::Events::Rule'
    Properties:
      ScheduleExpression: 'rate(5 minutes)'
      Targets:
        - Arn: !GetAtt WarmUpFunction.Arn
          Id: "WarmUpFunctionTarget"
  PermissionForEventsToInvokeLambda:
    Type: 'AWS::Lambda::Permission'
    Properties:
      FunctionName: !Ref WarmUpFunction
```

```
      Action: 'lambda:InvokeFunction'

      Principal: 'events.amazonaws.com'
```

4. Provisioned Concurrency

Provisioned Concurrency in AWS Lambda pre-warms a set number of execution environments so that they are ready to respond immediately.

```yaml
# Example of AWS CloudFormation configuration for provisioned concurrency

MyLambdaFunction:
  Type: 'AWS::Lambda::Function'
  Properties:
    FunctionName: 'myLambdaFunction'
    Handler: 'index.handler'
    Runtime: 'nodejs14.x'
    Role: !GetAtt LambdaExecutionRole.Arn
    Code:
      S3Bucket: 'example-bucket'
```

```
        S3Key: 'example-key'
  MyLambdaProvisionedConcurrency:
    Type: 'AWS::Lambda::Alias'
    Properties:
      FunctionName: !Ref MyLambdaFunction
      FunctionVersion: !GetAtt MyLambdaFunction.Version
      Name: 'provisioned'
      ProvisionedConcurrencyConfig:
        ProvisionedConcurrentExecutions: 10
```

5. Lazy Initialization

Initialize resources only when needed. For instance, database connections and clients can be created upon first use rather than at startup.

```javascript
let s3 = null;

exports.handler = async (event) => {
  if (s3 === null) {
```

```
    s3 = new (require('aws-sdk')).S3();
  }
  const params = {
    Bucket: 'example-bucket',
    Key: 'example-key'
  };
  const data = await s3.getObject(params).promise();
  return data.Body.toString();
};
```

6. Optimized Runtime Environment

Using an optimized runtime environment can significantly reduce cold start times. For instance, AWS Lambda provides different runtimes, and some, like Node.js or Python, typically have faster cold starts compared to others like Java or .NET.

```python
# Example of a Python Lambda function with minimal dependencies

import boto3
```

```python
def lambda_handler(event, context):
    s3 = boto3.client('s3')
    response = s3.get_object(Bucket='example-bucket', Key='example-key')
    data = response['Body'].read().decode('utf-8')
    return data
```

7. Container-based Functions

Container-based functions, such as AWS Lambda's container images, offer more control over the runtime environment, allowing for further optimizations such as custom initialization scripts and caching within the container.

```Dockerfile
# Example of a Dockerfile for an AWS Lambda function
FROM public.ecr.aws/lambda/python:3.8
COPY app.py ${LAMBDA_TASK_ROOT}
CMD ["app.lambda_handler"]
```

Architectural Patterns to Mitigate Cold Starts

1. **Microservices Architecture**

Designing functions following microservices architecture principles can isolate cold starts to specific services, reducing the impact on the overall system.

2. **Event-driven Architecture**

Using an event-driven architecture with asynchronous processing can help mitigate the effect of cold starts. Events can be queued and processed when the function is ready, smoothing out peaks and handling latency gracefully.

```yaml
# Example of an AWS CloudFormation configuration for event-driven Lambda functions
S3Bucket:
  Type: 'AWS::S3::Bucket'
S3EventFunction:
  Type: 'AWS::Lambda::Function'
  Properties:
    Handler: 'index.handler'
    Runtime: 'nodejs14.x'
    Role: !GetAtt LambdaExecutionRole.Arn
```

Code:

```
S3Bucket: 'example-bucket'
S3Key: 'example-key'
Events:
  S3BucketEvent:
    Type: 'S3'
    Properties:
      Bucket: !Ref S3Bucket
      Events: 's3:ObjectCreated:*'
```

3. CQRS and Event Sourcing

The Command Query Responsibility Segregation (CQRS) and Event Sourcing patterns can help handle cold starts by separating read and write operations and ensuring that the state is rebuilt from events, allowing for more resilient and responsive systems.

Handling cold starts is crucial for optimizing the performance of serverless functions. By minimizing function code size, optimizing dependencies, employing warm-up strategies, using provisioned concurrency, initializing resources lazily, leveraging optimized runtimes, and utilizing container-based functions, developers can significantly reduce cold start times. Architectural patterns such as microservices, event-driven architectures, and CQRS further enhance resilience and performance in scalable serverless systems. By carefully implementing these strategies, organizations can ensure that their serverless applications are both efficient and responsive, providing a better user experience.

Chapter 10

Serverless Cost Optimization Strategies: Building Efficient Systems

Cost-Effective Design Principles: Minimizing Resource Consumption

Serverless computing offers a compelling value proposition by abstracting infrastructure management and charging based on actual usage. However, to fully leverage the cost benefits of serverless architectures, it is crucial to design applications with resource consumption in mind. This article explores cost-effective design principles for minimizing resource consumption in serverless systems, supported by code examples and scalable software architecture patterns.

Understanding Resource Consumption in Serverless

In serverless computing, costs are driven by factors such as the number of function invocations, execution duration, memory allocation, and data transfer. The following principles focus on optimizing these factors to achieve cost efficiency.

Principles for Minimizing Resource Consumption

1. Optimize Function Execution Time

Reducing the execution time of serverless functions is critical for cost savings. Here are some strategies:

- **Efficient Algorithms:** Use algorithms with lower computational complexity to handle tasks more quickly.

- **Code Optimization:** Write efficient code to minimize execution time.

```python
# Python example of optimized code for string reversal
def lambda_handler(event, context):
    input_string = event['input_string']
    reversed_string = input_string[::-1]  # More efficient than using a loop
    return {'reversed_string': reversed_string}
```

- **Concurrency and Parallelism:** Utilize parallel processing to handle tasks simultaneously, reducing overall execution time.

```javascript
// Node.js example using Promise.all for parallel processing
const aws = require('aws-sdk');
```

```
const s3 = new aws.S3();

exports.handler = async (event) => {
  const keys = event.keys;
  const promises = keys.map(key => s3.getObject({ Bucket: 'example-bucket', Key: key }).promise());
  const results = await Promise.all(promises);
  return results.map(result => result.Body.toString());
};
```

2. Right-size Memory Allocation

Memory allocation affects both performance and cost. Allocating more memory can improve performance by providing more CPU power, but it also increases costs. Finding the optimal balance is key.

- **Memory Tuning:** Experiment with different memory sizes to find the most cost-effective allocation.

```bash
# AWS CLI command to update Lambda memory size
aws lambda update-function-configuration --function-name myFunction --memory-size 512
```

3. Reduce Function Invocation Frequency

Minimizing the number of invocations can significantly reduce costs.

- **Batch Processing:** Process multiple records in a single invocation instead of invoking the function for each record.

```javascript
// Example of batch processing in Node.js
exports.handler = async (event) => {
  const records = event.Records;
  for (const record of records) {
    // Process each record
  }
}
```

- **Event Filtering:** Use event filters to trigger functions only for relevant events.

```yaml
# AWS CloudFormation example with S3 event filtering
S3Bucket:
  Type: 'AWS::S3::Bucket'

S3EventFunction:
```

```
Type: 'AWS::Lambda::Function'
Properties:
  Handler: 'index.handler'
  Runtime: 'nodejs14.x'
  Role: !GetAtt LambdaExecutionRole.Arn
  Code:
    S3Bucket: 'example-bucket'
    S3Key: 'example-key'
  Events:
    S3BucketEvent:
      Type: 'S3'
      Properties:
        Bucket: !Ref S3Bucket
        Events: 's3:ObjectCreated:*'
        Filter:
          S3Key:
            Rules:
              - Name: 'suffix'
                Value: '.jpg'
```

4. Optimize Data Transfer

Data transfer costs can add up, especially for large datasets or high-frequency data transfers.

- **Data Compression:** Compress data before transferring to reduce the amount of data sent.

```python
# Python example of compressing data before uploading to S3
import boto3
import gzip
import json

def lambda_handler(event, context):
    s3 = boto3.client('s3')
    data = json.dumps(event)
    compressed_data = gzip.compress(data.encode('utf-8'))
    s3.put_object(Bucket='example-bucket', Key='compressed-data.json.gz', Body=compressed_data)
```

- **Efficient Data Access:** Access only the necessary data instead of transferring large datasets.

```javascript
// Node.js example of efficient data access with S3
const aws = require('aws-sdk');
const s3 = new aws.S3();

exports.handler = async (event) => {
  const params = {
```

```
    Bucket: 'example-bucket',
    Key: 'example-key',
    Range: 'bytes=0-1024' // Access only the first 1024 bytes
  };
  const data = await s3.getObject(params).promise();
  return data.Body.toString();
};
```

5. Leverage Managed Services

Using managed services for common tasks can reduce the need for custom code, thus reducing execution time and costs.

- **Database Operations:** Use services like AWS DynamoDB, which provides a fully managed NoSQL database with built-in scaling.

```python
# Python example using AWS DynamoDB
import boto3

def lambda_handler(event, context):
    dynamodb = boto3.client('dynamodb')
    response = dynamodb.get_item(
        TableName='example-table',
```

```
        Key={'id': {'S': event['id']}}
    )
    return response['Item']
```

- **Message Queues:** Use managed message queues like AWS SQS to handle asynchronous communication between services.

```javascript
// Node.js example using AWS SQS
const aws = require('aws-sdk');
const sqs = new aws.SQS();

exports.handler = async (event) => {
  const params = {
    QueueUrl: 'https://sqs.us-east-1.amazonaws.com/123456789012/example-queue',
    MessageBody: JSON.stringify(event)
  };
  await sqs.sendMessage(params).promise();
  return { status: 'Message sent' };
};
```

Architectural Patterns for Cost Efficiency

1. Microservices Architecture

Breaking down an application into microservices can isolate high-resource components, allowing independent scaling and optimization.

- **Independent Scaling:** Scale each microservice independently based on demand, reducing overall resource consumption.

```yaml
# Example of AWS CloudFormation configuration for independent scaling
ServiceAFunction:
  Type: 'AWS::Lambda::Function'
  Properties:
    FunctionName: 'serviceAFunction'
    Handler: 'index.handler'
    Runtime: 'nodejs14.x'
    MemorySize: 256
    Role: !GetAtt LambdaExecutionRole.Arn
    Code:
      S3Bucket: 'example-bucket'
      S3Key: 'serviceA-key'

ServiceBFunction:
  Type: 'AWS::Lambda::Function'
  Properties:
    FunctionName: 'serviceBFunction'
```

```
      Handler: 'index.handler'
      Runtime: 'nodejs14.x'
      MemorySize: 512
      Role: !GetAtt LambdaExecutionRole.Arn
      Code:
        S3Bucket: 'example-bucket'
        S3Key: 'serviceB-key'
```

2. Event-Driven Architecture

Using event-driven architecture can decouple services and allow them to process events asynchronously, optimizing resource usage.

- **Asynchronous Processing:** Use message queues or event streams to handle tasks asynchronously, smoothing out peaks and reducing resource contention.

```yaml
# AWS CloudFormation example with S3 and SQS for asynchronous processing
S3Bucket:
  Type: 'AWS::S3::Bucket'

S3EventQueue:
  Type: 'AWS::SQS::Queue'
```

```
  Properties:
    QueueName: 's3-event-queue'

S3EventFunction:
  Type: 'AWS::Lambda::Function'
  Properties:
    Handler: 'index.handler'
    Runtime: 'nodejs14.x'
    Role: !GetAtt LambdaExecutionRole.Arn
    Code:
      S3Bucket: 'example-bucket'
      S3Key: 'example-key'
    Events:
      S3BucketEvent:
        Type: 'S3'
        Properties:
          Bucket: !Ref S3Bucket
          Events: 's3:ObjectCreated:*'
          Queue: !Ref S3EventQueue
```

3. Serverless Frameworks

Utilize serverless frameworks and infrastructure-as-code (IaC) tools to automate deployments, ensure consistency, and optimize resource configurations.

- **Serverless Framework:** Use frameworks like the Serverless Framework to define and deploy serverless applications.

```yaml
# serverless.yml configuration for the Serverless Framework
service: example-service

provider:
  name: aws
  runtime: nodejs14.x

functions:
  hello:
    handler: handler.hello
    events:
      - http:
          path: hello
          method: get

resources:
  Resources:
    S3Bucket:
      Type: 'AWS::S3::Bucket'
```

Minimizing resource consumption in serverless systems is essential for cost-effective design. By optimizing function execution time, right-sizing memory allocation, reducing invocation frequency, optimizing data transfer, and leveraging managed services, developers can significantly reduce costs. Employing architectural patterns such as microservices, event-driven architecture, and serverless frameworks further enhances the scalability and cost-efficiency of serverless applications. Careful design and optimization can ensure that serverless solutions provide both economic and operational benefits.

Monitoring and Analyzing Costs: Identifying Areas for Improvement in Serverless Systems

In serverless computing, where resources are abstracted away and billed based on actual usage, keeping track of costs and identifying areas for improvement is critical. Effective cost monitoring and analysis can help optimize spending, improve performance, and ensure the financial sustainability of serverless applications. This article explores techniques and tools for monitoring and analyzing costs, supported by code examples and scalable software architecture patterns.

Importance of Cost Monitoring

Monitoring costs in a serverless environment involves tracking various metrics such as invocation counts, execution duration, memory usage, and data transfer. Understanding these metrics allows organizations to pinpoint inefficiencies, optimize resource usage, and ultimately reduce costs.

Tools for Cost Monitoring and Analysis

1. AWS Cost Explorer

AWS Cost Explorer helps visualize and manage AWS costs. It provides detailed insights into spending patterns and identifies cost drivers.

- **Usage Reports:** Generate reports to analyze cost trends and pinpoint areas for optimization.

- **Cost Allocation Tags:** Use tags to categorize and track costs by project, team, or department.

```yaml
# AWS CloudFormation configuration for enabling cost allocation tags
AWSTaggingPolicy:
  Type: 'AWS::IAM::Policy'
  Properties:
    PolicyName: 'CostAllocationTagsPolicy'
```

```yaml
      PolicyDocument:
        Version: '2012-10-17'
        Statement:
          - Effect: 'Allow'
            Action:
              - 'tag:GetResources'
              - 'tag:TagResources'
            Resource: '*'
      Roles:
        - !Ref LambdaExecutionRole
```

2. AWS CloudWatch

AWS CloudWatch provides monitoring and observability for AWS resources. It tracks metrics, logs, and events, making it a powerful tool for cost analysis.

- **Custom Metrics:** Create custom metrics to monitor specific aspects of serverless functions.

- **Alarms**: Set up alarms to notify you when costs exceed predefined thresholds.

```javascript
// Example of sending custom metrics to CloudWatch in Node.js
const AWS = require('aws-sdk');
```

```
const cloudwatch = new AWS.CloudWatch();

exports.handler = async (event) => {
  const params = {
    MetricData: [
      {
        MetricName: 'InvocationCount',
        Dimensions: [
          {
            Name: 'FunctionName',
            Value: 'myLambdaFunction'
          }

        Unit: 'Count',
        Value: 1
      }

    Namespace: 'MyServerlessApp'
  };

  await cloudwatch.putMetricData(params).promise();
  return { status: 'Metric sent' };
};
```
```

### 3. AWS Lambda Power Tuning
```

AWS Lambda Power Tuning is an open-source tool that helps find the optimal memory configuration for your Lambda functions to minimize cost and maximize performance.

```bash
# Install the AWS Lambda Power Tuning tool
npm install -g aws-lambda-power-tuning

# Run the power tuning tool
lambda-power-tuning -m 128,256,512,1024,1536,3008 -n MyLambdaFunction
```

Analyzing Cost Data

Analyzing cost data involves identifying patterns, understanding cost drivers, and finding areas for optimization.

1. Break Down Costs by Service

Understanding which services contribute most to your costs can help identify where to focus optimization efforts. Use AWS Cost Explorer to generate detailed reports.

```yaml
```

```
# AWS CloudFormation configuration for a detailed billing report
DetailedBillingReport:
  Type: 'AWS::S3::BucketPolicy'
  Properties:
    Bucket: !Ref BillingBucket
    PolicyDocument:
      Version: '2012-10-17'
      Statement:
        - Effect: 'Allow'
          Action:
            - 's3:GetBucketAcl'
            - 's3:PutObject'
          Resource: !Sub 'arn:aws:s3:::${BillingBucket}/*'
        - Effect: 'Allow'
          Action:
            - 's3:GetBucketPolicy'
          Resource: !Sub 'arn:aws:s3:::${BillingBucket}'
```

2. Identify High-Usage Functions

Identify Lambda functions with high invocation counts or long execution times. Use AWS CloudWatch to track these metrics and analyze logs for insights.

```javascript
// Example of logging execution duration in Node.js
```

```javascript
exports.handler = async (event) => {
  const startTime = Date.now();
  // Function logic
  const endTime = Date.now();
  console.log(`Execution duration: ${endTime - startTime}ms`);
  return { status: 'Function executed' };
};
```

3. Optimize Resource Allocation

Once high-usage functions are identified, analyze their memory allocation and execution duration to find the optimal balance.

```yaml
# AWS CloudFormation configuration for optimizing Lambda memory allocation
OptimizedLambdaFunction:
  Type: 'AWS::Lambda::Function'
  Properties:
    FunctionName: 'optimizedLambdaFunction'
    Handler: 'index.handler'
    Runtime: 'nodejs14.x'
    MemorySize: 512  # Adjust based on analysis
    Timeout: 30
    Role: !GetAtt LambdaExecutionRole.Arn
```

```
Code:
  S3Bucket: 'example-bucket'
  S3Key: 'example-key'
```

4. Use Cost-Effective Storage Solutions

Evaluate the cost-effectiveness of your storage solutions. For example, consider using Amazon S3 Infrequent Access (IA) or Glacier for storing less frequently accessed data.

```python
# Python example of moving data to S3 Glacier
import boto3

def lambda_handler(event, context):
    s3 = boto3.client('s3')
    copy_source = {'Bucket': 'example-bucket', 'Key': 'example-key'}
    s3.copy_object(
        Bucket='example-bucket',
        CopySource=copy_source,
        Key='example-key',
        StorageClass='GLACIER'
    )
    return {'status': 'Object moved to Glacier'}
```

Scalable Architectural Patterns for Cost Efficiency

1. Microservices Architecture

Microservices architecture breaks down applications into small, loosely coupled services. This allows independent scaling and cost optimization for each service.

- **Service Isolation:** Isolate high-cost services to analyze and optimize them separately.

- **Independent Scaling:** Scale each microservice based on its specific demand, reducing overall costs.

```yaml
# Example of AWS CloudFormation configuration for microservices
ServiceAFunction:
  Type: 'AWS::Lambda::Function'
  Properties:
    FunctionName: 'serviceAFunction'
    Handler: 'index.handler'
    Runtime: 'nodejs14.x'
    MemorySize: 256
    Timeout: 30
    Role: !GetAtt LambdaExecutionRole.Arn
```

```
      Code:
        S3Bucket: 'example-bucket'
        S3Key: 'serviceA-key'

  ServiceBFunction:
    Type: 'AWS::Lambda::Function'
    Properties:
      FunctionName: 'serviceBFunction'
      Handler: 'index.handler'
      Runtime: 'nodejs14.x'
      MemorySize: 512
      Timeout: 60
      Role: !GetAtt LambdaExecutionRole.Arn
      Code:
        S3Bucket: 'example-bucket'
        S3Key: 'serviceB-key'
```
```

## 2. Event-Driven Architecture

Event-driven architecture decouples services, allowing them to respond to events asynchronously. This approach can lead to more efficient resource utilization and cost savings.

- **Asynchronous Processing:** Use message queues or event streams to handle tasks asynchronously,
```

smoothing out resource utilization and reducing peak loads.

```yaml
# AWS CloudFormation example with S3 and SQS for asynchronous processing
S3Bucket:
  Type: 'AWS::S3::Bucket'

S3EventQueue:
  Type: 'AWS::SQS::Queue'
  Properties:
    QueueName: 's3-event-queue'

S3EventFunction:
  Type: 'AWS::Lambda::Function'
  Properties:
    Handler: 'index.handler'
    Runtime: 'nodejs14.x'
    Role: !GetAtt LambdaExecutionRole.Arn
    Code:
      S3Bucket: 'example-bucket'
      S3Key: 'example-key'
    Events:
      S3BucketEvent:
        Type: 'S3'
        Properties:
          Bucket: !Ref S3Bucket
```

```
    Events: 's3:ObjectCreated:*'
    Queue: !Ref S3EventQueue
```

3. Serverless Frameworks

Using serverless frameworks and infrastructure-as-code (IaC) tools helps automate deployments, ensure consistency, and optimize resource configurations.

- **Serverless Framework:** Use frameworks like the Serverless Framework to define and deploy serverless applications efficiently.

```yaml
# serverless.yml configuration for the Serverless Framework
service: example-service

provider:
  name: aws
  runtime: nodejs14.x

functions:
  hello:
    handler: handler.hello
    events:
      - http:
```

```
      path: hello
      method: get

resources:
  Resources:
    S3Bucket:
      Type: 'AWS::S3::Bucket'
```

Monitoring and analyzing costs in serverless systems is essential for maintaining cost-efficiency and optimizing resource usage. By leveraging tools such as AWS Cost Explorer, AWS CloudWatch, and AWS Lambda Power Tuning, organizations can gain valuable insights into their spending patterns and identify areas for improvement. Employing scalable architectural patterns like microservices, event-driven architecture, and serverless frameworks further enhances cost management. Through careful cost monitoring and analysis, businesses can ensure that their serverless applications are both economically sustainable and highly performant.

Right-Sizing Resources: Choosing the Right Function Type and Memory Allocation

As cloud computing evolves, serverless architectures have become increasingly popular due to their scalability, cost-effectiveness, and reduced operational complexity. Serverless computing, exemplified by platforms like AWS Lambda, Azure Functions, and Google Cloud Functions, allows developers to focus on code rather than managing infrastructure. However, one crucial aspect of optimizing serverless applications involves right-sizing resources—choosing the appropriate function type and memory allocation to ensure performance and cost-efficiency. This article explores strategies for achieving this, accompanied by relevant code examples and considerations based on scalable software architecture patterns.

Understanding Serverless Functions

Serverless functions are event-driven, stateless functions that execute in response to specific triggers, such as HTTP requests, database changes, or scheduled events. These functions scale automatically based on the workload, eliminating the need for manual intervention in resource management. However, developers must configure memory allocation and function types to optimize performance and cost.

Memory Allocation

Memory allocation in serverless functions is crucial because it directly impacts both performance and cost. Most serverless platforms allow you to allocate memory in increments (e.g., from 128 MB to 10 GB in AWS Lambda). The allocated memory also affects CPU, network, and I/O resources; more memory typically means more CPU power.

Example: AWS Lambda Memory Allocation

Consider a Python function deployed on AWS Lambda that processes images. Here's an example of how you might configure memory allocation:

```python
import boto3

import os

from PIL import Image

s3 = boto3.client('s3')

def lambda_handler(event, context):

    bucket = event['Records'][0]['s3']['bucket']['name']

    key = event['Records'][0]['s3']['object']['key']

    # Download image from S3

    download_path = '/tmp/{}{}'.format(uuid.uuid4(), os.path.basename(key))

    s3.download_file(bucket, key, download_path)

    # Process image

    with Image.open(download_path) as img:

        img = img.resize((img.width // 2, img.height // 2))
```

```
        output_path = '/tmp/resized-{}'.format(os.path.basename(key))

        img.save(output_path)

    # Upload processed image back to S3

    s3.upload_file(output_path, bucket, 'resized/{}'.format(key))

    return {

        'statusCode': 200,

        'body': json.dumps('Image processed successfully')

    }
```

For this image processing task, memory allocation significantly impacts performance. If the function runs slowly, you might need to increase memory allocation. AWS Lambda pricing is proportional to the memory allocated and the execution time. Therefore, finding the optimal memory allocation involves balancing performance improvements against cost increases.

Choosing the Right Function Type

Choosing the right function type involves selecting appropriate triggers and execution contexts based on the application's requirements. Common function types include:

1. HTTP Triggered Functions: Suitable for REST APIs and webhooks.

2. Event-Driven Functions: Respond to events from services like S3, DynamoDB, or Kinesis.

3. Scheduled Functions: Run at specified intervals, akin to cron jobs.

4. Queue-Triggered Functions: Process messages from queues like SQS or RabbitMQ.

Example: HTTP Triggered Function

Here's an example of an HTTP-triggered function using AWS Lambda with API Gateway:

```python
import json

def lambda_handler(event, context):
    body = {
        "message": "Hello, world!"
    }
    response = {
        "statusCode": 200,
        "body": json.dumps(body)
```

        }

    return response

```

This simple function returns a JSON response to HTTP requests. For web applications or APIs, HTTP-triggered functions are ideal. They can scale automatically based on the number of incoming requests.

## Scalable Software Architecture Patterns for Serverless Systems

Implementing scalable software architecture patterns is essential for building robust serverless applications. Key patterns include:

**1. Microservices Architecture:** Decomposing applications into small, independent services that can be developed, deployed, and scaled independently.

**2. Event-Driven Architecture:** Using events to trigger functions, enabling loosely coupled services that react to changes in real-time.

**3. Queue-Based Load Leveling:** Using queues to buffer requests, ensuring that functions can handle bursts of traffic without being overwhelmed.

**4. Function Composition:** Chaining functions together to perform complex workflows, often orchestrated using tools like AWS Step Functions.
```

Example: Event-Driven Architecture

In an event-driven architecture, functions react to events, allowing for real-time processing and scalability. Consider a serverless application that processes user uploads to S3 and updates a database.

```python
import json
import boto3
from datetime import datetime

dynamodb = boto3.resource('dynamodb')
table = dynamodb.Table('Uploads')

def lambda_handler(event, context):
    bucket = event['Records'][0]['s3']['bucket']['name']
    key = event['Records'][0]['s3']['object']['key']
    timestamp = datetime.utcnow().isoformat()

    # Update DynamoDB with the new upload information
    table.put_item(
        Item={
```

```
        'upload_id': key,

        'bucket': bucket,

        'timestamp': timestamp

    }

    return {

        'statusCode': 200,

        'body': json.dumps('Database updated successfully')

    }
```

In this example, the function is triggered by an S3 event whenever a new object is uploaded. It updates a DynamoDB table with the upload details, demonstrating how event-driven architectures can enable real-time data processing.

Optimizing Memory Allocation and Function Types

To right-size resources effectively, follow these steps:

1. Profile Your Functions: Use profiling tools provided by the cloud provider (e.g., AWS CloudWatch, Azure Monitor) to gather performance data. Identify bottlenecks and resource usage patterns.

2. Experiment with Different Memory Allocations: Start with a baseline memory allocation and incrementally increase it, monitoring performance improvements and cost changes.

3. Choose Appropriate Function Types: Match function types to use cases. For instance, use queue-triggered functions for batch processing and HTTP-triggered functions for APIs.

4. Implement Best Practices: Follow best practices such as minimizing cold start latency, reusing connections, and optimizing code for performance.

5. Monitor and Iterate: Continuously monitor performance and costs, adjusting memory allocations and function configurations as needed.

Example: Memory Allocation Optimization

Suppose you have a data processing function that takes varying amounts of time depending on the memory allocated. Here's how you might approach optimizing memory allocation:

1. Initial Configuration: Start with a lower memory allocation (e.g., 256 MB).

2. Profile Performance: Use AWS CloudWatch to measure execution time and memory usage.

3. Incremental Adjustments: Increase memory allocation in steps (e.g., 512 MB, 1024 MB) and monitor the impact on execution time.

4. Cost Analysis: Calculate the cost for each configuration, considering both memory allocation and execution time.

```python
import time

def data_processing_function(event, context):
    start_time = time.time()
    # Simulate data processing task
    time.sleep(2)  # Placeholder for actual processing logic
    end_time = time.time()
    execution_time = end_time - start_time
    return {
        'statusCode': 200,
        'body': json.dumps(f'Execution time: {execution_time} seconds')
    }
```

By following these steps, you can identify the optimal memory allocation that provides the best performance at the lowest cost.

Right-sizing resources in serverless architectures is a critical task that balances performance and cost. By carefully choosing the right function type and memory allocation, you can optimize your serverless applications for scalability and efficiency. Profiling your functions, experimenting with different configurations, and leveraging scalable software architecture patterns like microservices, event-driven architectures, and queue-based load leveling are key strategies. With continuous monitoring and iteration, you can ensure that your serverless applications are both performant and cost-effective, meeting the demands of modern cloud-native environments.

Chapter 11

Security Best Practices for Serverless: Authentication, Authorization, and Encryption

Serverless computing offers numerous benefits, including scalability, reduced operational overhead, and cost-efficiency. However, ensuring security in serverless architectures is paramount due to the shared responsibility model between the cloud provider and the application owner. In this article, we'll delve into security best practices for serverless applications, focusing on authentication, authorization, and encryption. We'll explore how to implement these practices using scalable software architecture patterns and provide code examples for illustration.

Authentication

Authentication is the process of verifying the identity of users or systems attempting to access resources. In serverless architectures, authentication ensures that only authorized entities can invoke functions or access sensitive data.

Best Practices

1. Use Identity Providers: Leverage identity providers like Amazon Cognito, Auth0, or Azure Active Directory to manage user authentication. These services offer features such as user management, multi-factor authentication (MFA), and social identity providers.

2. API Gateway Authentication: Secure APIs deployed with AWS Lambda or Azure Functions using API Gateway authentication mechanisms such as API keys, IAM (AWS Identity and Access Management) authentication, or OAuth 2.0.

3. JWT (JSON Web Tokens): Implement JWT-based authentication for stateless authentication between client and serverless functions. JWT tokens contain encoded information about the user's identity and can be validated without server-side state.

Example: JWT Authentication in AWS Lambda

```python
import jwt

def lambda_handler(event, context):
    token = event['headers']['Authorization']
    
    # Verify JWT token
    try:
```

```
        decoded_token = jwt.decode(token, 'secret',
algorithms=['HS256'])
        user_id = decoded_token['user_id']
        # Proceed with authorized logic
        return {
            'statusCode': 200,
            'body': f'Welcome, user {user_id}!'
        }
    except jwt.ExpiredSignatureError:
        return {
            'statusCode': 401,
            'body': 'Token has expired'
        }
    except jwt.InvalidTokenError:
        return {
            'statusCode': 401,
            'body': 'Invalid token'
        }
```
```

In this example, the AWS Lambda function validates a JWT token extracted from the HTTP headers. If the token is valid, it proceeds with the authorized logic; otherwise, it returns an authentication error.

**Authorization**
```

Authorization determines what authenticated users or systems are allowed to do within an application. It involves defining and enforcing access control policies to restrict access to resources based on user roles, permissions, or other attributes.

Best Practices

1. Role-Based Access Control (RBAC: Implement RBAC to assign permissions to users or roles based on their organizational roles or responsibilities. Use IAM roles in AWS or Azure Active Directory roles in Azure to manage access at scale.

2. Fine-Grained Access Control: Apply granular access controls to resources, restricting access to specific operations or data fields based on user attributes or conditions.

3. Attribute-Based Access Control (ABAC): Use ABAC to define access policies based on user attributes such as department, location, or job title. This allows for dynamic, context-aware access control.

Example: Role-Based Access Control in Azure Functions

```python
```

```python
import azure.functions as func

def main(req: func.HttpRequest, context: func.Context) -> func.HttpResponse:
    # Validate user role
    user_role = req.headers.get('X-User-Role')

    if user_role == 'admin':
        # Authorized logic for admin user
        return func.HttpResponse("Welcome, admin!", status_code=200)
    else:
        return func.HttpResponse("Unauthorized", status_code=403)
```

In this Azure Functions example, the function checks the `X-User-Role` header to determine the user's role. If the user is an admin, it allows access; otherwise, it returns an unauthorized response.

Encryption

Encryption protects data at rest and in transit, safeguarding it from unauthorized access or tampering. In serverless architectures, encryption is essential for securing sensitive data stored in databases, transmitted over networks, or processed by functions.

Best Practices

1. Data Encryption at Rest: Encrypt data stored in databases or object storage using encryption mechanisms provided by the cloud provider, such as AWS KMS (Key Management Service) or Azure Key Vault.

2. Transport Layer Security (TLS): Encrypt data transmitted over networks using TLS/SSL protocols to prevent eavesdropping and man-in-the-middle attacks.

3. Client-Side Encryption: Implement client-side encryption for sensitive data before sending it to serverless functions. This ensures data confidentiality even if the backend is compromised.

Example: Data Encryption in AWS Lambda with KMS

```python
import boto3

kms = boto3.client('kms')

def encrypt_data(data):
    response = kms.encrypt(
        KeyId='alias/my-key',
```

```
    Plaintext=data.encode('utf-8')
)
encrypted_data = response['CiphertextBlob']
return encrypted_data
```
```

In this AWS Lambda function, sensitive data is encrypted using the AWS Key Management Service (KMS) before storing or transmitting it. The `encrypt_data` function encrypts the plaintext data using a KMS key specified by its alias.

Security is a critical aspect of serverless architectures, requiring careful consideration and implementation of authentication, authorization, and encryption mechanisms. By following best practices and leveraging scalable software architecture patterns, developers can build secure serverless applications that protect against threats and vulnerabilities. Authentication mechanisms like JWT tokens, role-based access control (RBAC), and encryption techniques such as data encryption at rest and in transit play crucial roles in ensuring the confidentiality, integrity, and availability of serverless applications. As serverless adoption continues to grow, prioritizing security will be essential to mitigate risks and build trust in cloud-native environments.
```

Securing APIs and Functions: Protecting Your Endpoints and Data

Securing APIs and functions in serverless architectures is crucial for protecting sensitive data and preventing unauthorized access. As serverless computing continues to gain popularity, ensuring robust security measures becomes paramount. In this article, we'll explore best practices for securing APIs and functions in serverless systems, focusing on endpoint protection and data security. We'll provide code examples and discuss scalable software architecture patterns to illustrate these concepts effectively.

Endpoint Protection

APIs serve as the entry points for serverless applications, making them a prime target for attackers. Endpoint protection involves implementing mechanisms to authenticate and authorize users, as well as safeguarding against common security threats such as injection attacks and denial-of-service (DoS) attacks.

Best Practices

1. Authentication: Use strong authentication mechanisms such as OAuth 2.0, JWT tokens, or API keys to verify the identity of clients accessing the API endpoints.

2. Authorization: Implement fine-grained access control to restrict access to API resources based on user roles, permissions, or other attributes.

3. Input Validation: Validate and sanitize input parameters to prevent injection attacks such as SQL injection or cross-site scripting (XSS).

4. Rate Limiting: Enforce rate limiting to prevent DoS attacks and protect against abuse of API endpoints.

5. HTTPS: Use HTTPS to encrypt data transmitted between clients and API endpoints, preventing eavesdropping and man-in-the-middle attacks.

Example: API Authentication with API Gateway and Lambda (AWS)

```python
import json

def lambda_handler(event, context):
    # Verify API key
    api_key = event['headers'].get('x-api-key')
```

```
    if api_key == 'YOUR_API_KEY':
        # Authorized logic
        return {
            'statusCode': 200,
            'body': json.dumps('Authenticated successfully')
        }
    else:
        return {
            'statusCode': 401,
            'body': json.dumps('Unauthorized')
        }
```

In this AWS Lambda function, the `x-api-key` header is used for API key authentication. If the provided API key matches the expected value, the client is authorized to access the API endpoint; otherwise, a 401 Unauthorized response is returned.

Data Security

Data security involves protecting sensitive information stored in databases, transmitted over networks, or processed by serverless functions. In serverless architectures, data security is essential due to the distributed nature of applications and the potential exposure of data to external threats.

Best Practices

1. Encryption at Rest: Encrypt data stored in databases or object storage using encryption mechanisms provided by the cloud provider, such as AWS KMS or Azure Key Vault.

2. Encryption in Transit: Encrypt data transmitted over networks using TLS/SSL protocols to prevent eavesdropping and interception.

3. Client-Side Encryption: Implement client-side encryption for sensitive data before transmitting it to serverless functions, ensuring data confidentiality even if the backend is compromised.

4. Data Masking: Mask sensitive data fields such as passwords or credit card numbers to prevent unauthorized access or exposure.

Example: Data Encryption in AWS Lambda with KMS

```python
import boto3

kms = boto3.client('kms')
```

```
def encrypt_data(data):
    response = kms.encrypt(
        KeyId='alias/my-key',
        Plaintext=data.encode('utf-8')
    )
    encrypted_data = response['CiphertextBlob']
    return encrypted_data
```
```

In this AWS Lambda function, sensitive data is encrypted using the AWS Key Management Service (KMS) before storing or transmitting it. The `encrypt_data` function encrypts the plaintext data using a KMS key specified by its alias.

## Scalable Software Architecture Patterns

Scalable software architecture patterns play a vital role in ensuring the security of serverless applications. By leveraging architectural patterns such as microservices, event-driven architectures, and serverless computing, developers can build secure and resilient systems that can scale to meet the demands of modern cloud environments.

## Microservices Architecture
```

Decompose applications into smaller, independent microservices, each with its own set of responsibilities and security boundaries. This allows for isolation of sensitive data and reduces the attack surface area.

Event-Driven Architecture

Use event-driven architectures to build loosely coupled systems that react to events in real-time. By decoupling components and using asynchronous communication, event-driven architectures enhance security by reducing the impact of failures and isolating potential security breaches.

Serverless Computing

Leverage serverless computing platforms like AWS Lambda, Azure Functions, or Google Cloud Functions to offload infrastructure management tasks and focus on building secure application logic. Serverless architectures benefit from built-in security features provided by the cloud provider, such as fine-grained access control and encryption at rest.

Securing APIs and functions in serverless architectures is essential for protecting sensitive data and preventing unauthorized access. By implementing authentication, authorization, and encryption mechanisms, developers can build secure applications that withstand external threats. Best practices such as input validation, rate limiting, and HTTPS encryption help mitigate common security risks associated with API endpoints. Similarly, data security measures such as encryption at rest, encryption in transit, and data masking ensure the confidentiality and integrity of sensitive information. Scalable software architecture patterns like microservices, event-driven architectures, and serverless computing further enhance security by promoting isolation, resilience, and scalability. As serverless adoption continues to grow, prioritizing security will be critical to building trust and ensuring the success of cloud-native applications.

Compliance Considerations: Building Secure Serverless Systems for Regulated Industries

In regulated industries such as healthcare, finance, and government, compliance with industry standards and regulations is paramount. When building serverless systems in these sectors, developers must ensure that their applications adhere to relevant compliance requirements while maintaining security and scalability. In this article, we'll explore compliance considerations for building secure serverless systems in regulated industries. We'll discuss best practices, provide code examples, and highlight scalable software architecture patterns to ensure compliance while meeting business objectives.

Regulatory Compliance in Serverless Systems

Regulated industries are subject to various compliance standards and regulations, including:

1. Healthcare (HIPAA): The Health Insurance Portability and Accountability Act (HIPAA) mandates strict controls for protecting electronic protected health information (ePHI) to ensure patient privacy and data security.

2. Finance (PCI DSS, GDPR): The Payment Card Industry Data Security Standard (PCI DSS) governs the handling of credit card data, while the General Data Protection Regulation (GDPR) regulates the processing and storage of personal data for EU citizens.

3. Government (FISMA, FedRAMP): The Federal Information Security Management Act (FISMA) and the Federal Risk and Authorization Management Program (FedRAMP) establish security standards for federal agencies and cloud service providers hosting government data.

When building serverless systems in these industries, developers must address compliance requirements related to data protection, access control, auditing, and risk management.

Compliance Best Practices

Data Encryption and Protection

1. Encryption at Rest: Encrypt sensitive data stored in databases or object storage using encryption mechanisms provided by the cloud provider (e.g., AWS KMS, Azure Key Vault).

2. Encryption in Transit: Encrypt data transmitted over networks using TLS/SSL protocols to prevent eavesdropping and interception.

3. Tokenization: Tokenize sensitive data such as credit card numbers to reduce the risk of exposure in the event of a breach.

Access Control and Authentication

1. Role-Based Access Control (RBAC): Implement RBAC to assign permissions to users based on their roles and responsibilities.

2. Multi-Factor Authentication (MFA): Enforce MFA for user authentication to provide an additional layer of security.

3. API Key Management: Manage API keys securely and rotate them regularly to prevent unauthorized access.

Audit Logging and Monitoring

1. Audit Trails: Implement comprehensive audit logging to track user access, data modifications, and system activities.

2. Monitoring and Alerting: Use monitoring tools (e.g., AWS CloudWatch, Azure Monitor) to monitor system performance, security events, and compliance violations. Set up alerts for suspicious activities or policy violations.

Example: HIPAA-Compliant Serverless Function (AWS Lambda)

```python
import boto3
import json

def lambda_handler(event, context):
    # Extract sensitive data from event
    patient_id = event['patient_id']
```

```
    medical_history = event['medical_history']

    # Encrypt sensitive data using AWS KMS
    kms = boto3.client('kms')
    encrypted_medical_history = kms.encrypt(
        KeyId='alias/my-key',
        Plaintext=medical_history.encode('utf-8')
    )['CiphertextBlob']

    # Store encrypted data in database
    # (Database and storage configuration omitted for brevity)

    return {
        'statusCode': 200,
        'body': json.dumps('Data stored securely')
    }
```

In this example, a serverless function processes medical data in compliance with HIPAA regulations. The function encrypts sensitive medical history information using AWS Key Management Service (KMS) before storing it in a database, ensuring data protection and confidentiality.

Scalable Software Architecture Patterns

Scalable software architecture patterns play a crucial role in building secure and compliant serverless systems. Here are some patterns to consider:

1. Microservices Architecture: Decompose applications into smaller, independent microservices, each with its own set of responsibilities and security boundaries. This promotes isolation and reduces the impact of security breaches.

2. Event-Driven Architecture: Use event-driven architectures to build loosely coupled systems that react to events in real-time. By decoupling components and using asynchronous communication, event-driven architectures enhance security and scalability.

3. Serverless Computing: Leverage serverless computing platforms such as AWS Lambda, Azure Functions, or Google Cloud Functions to offload infrastructure management tasks and focus on building secure application logic. Serverless architectures benefit from built-in security features provided by the cloud provider, such as fine-grained access control and encryption at rest.

Compliance considerations are paramount when building serverless systems for regulated industries. By adhering to industry standards and regulations such as HIPAA,

PCI DSS, and GDPR, developers can ensure the security and privacy of sensitive data while meeting compliance requirements. Best practices such as data encryption, access control, audit logging, and monitoring help mitigate risks and ensure that serverless systems operate in a secure and compliant manner. Scalable software architecture patterns such as microservices, event-driven architectures, and serverless computing further enhance security and scalability, enabling organizations to build robust and compliant applications in regulated industries. As serverless adoption continues to grow, prioritizing compliance and security will be essential for building trust and maintaining regulatory compliance.

Chapter 12

Serverless on the Edge: Bringing Computing Closer to the Data

In today's digital landscape, where data is generated at an unprecedented rate, the demand for efficient, scalable, and low-latency computing solutions is higher than ever. Traditional cloud computing paradigms often struggle to meet these demands, especially when it comes to applications requiring real-time processing or operating in geographically distributed environments. This is where serverless on the edge comes into play. By bringing computing closer to the data source, serverless on the edge enables faster processing, reduced latency, and enhanced scalability. In this article, we'll explore the concept of serverless on the edge, discuss its benefits, and delve into scalable software architecture patterns for building serverless systems.

What is Serverless on the Edge?

Serverless on the edge refers to the deployment of serverless computing resources closer to the data source, typically at the network edge. Unlike traditional cloud computing, where applications are hosted in centralized data centers, serverless on the edge leverages a distributed infrastructure to bring computing resources closer to end-users and devices. This proximity reduces the distance data needs to travel, resulting in lower latency and improved performance for latency-sensitive applications.

Benefits of Serverless on the Edge:

1. Low Latency: By processing data closer to the source, serverless on the edge minimizes the time it takes for data to travel between the client and the server. This reduction in latency is crucial for real-time applications such as IoT devices, gaming platforms, and multimedia streaming services.

2. Scalability: Serverless architectures inherently offer scalability by automatically provisioning and managing resources based on demand. When combined with edge computing, this scalability is further enhanced, as resources can be dynamically allocated and de-allocated at the network edge, ensuring optimal performance even during periods of peak usage.

3. Cost Efficiency: Serverless on the edge can be more cost-effective than traditional cloud computing models, as it eliminates the need to maintain and manage infrastructure in centralized data centers. Additionally, since resources are provisioned on-demand, organizations only pay for the computing resources they actually use, rather than for idle capacity.

Scalable Software Architecture Patterns for Serverless Systems:

1. Event-Driven Architecture:

Event-driven architecture (EDA) is a software design pattern that emphasizes the production, detection, consumption, and reaction to events. In a serverless context, EDA is well-suited for handling asynchronous communication between distributed components. Events can trigger serverless functions deployed at the network edge, enabling real-time processing of data close to the source.

Example Code:

```python
# Define an event handler function
def event_handler(event, context):
    # Process incoming event
    data = event['data']
    # Perform computation or invoke other services
    result = process_data(data)
    return result
```

```
# Deploy the event handler function as a serverless
function
```

2. Microservices Architecture:

Microservices architecture decomposes an application into smaller, independently deployable services that are organized around specific business capabilities. When combined with serverless computing on the edge, microservices enable greater flexibility, scalability, and fault isolation. Each microservice can be deployed as a serverless function at the network edge, allowing for distributed processing and seamless scalability.

Example Code:

```python
# Define microservice functions
def user_service(event, context):
    # Handle user-related operations
    ...

def product_service(event, context):
    # Handle product-related operations
    ...

# Deploy microservices as serverless functions
```

```

### 3. Content Delivery Networks (CDNs):

Content Delivery Networks (CDNs) are distributed networks of servers that deliver web content to users based on their geographic location. By caching content at edge locations, CDNs reduce latency and improve the performance of web applications. When combined with serverless computing, CDNs can be used to deploy serverless functions at edge locations, enabling dynamic content generation and personalized user experiences.

**Example Code:**

```python
# Define CDN edge function
def cdn_edge_function(event, context):
    # Retrieve cached content or generate dynamic content
    ...
    return content

# Deploy CDN edge function as a serverless function
```

Serverless on the edge represents a paradigm shift in the way we architect and deploy applications, offering lower latency, improved scalability, and cost efficiency. By
```

bringing computing closer to the data source, organizations can deliver faster, more responsive applications to end-users and devices. Leveraging scalable software architecture patterns such as event-driven architecture, microservices, and content delivery networks, developers can build robust, distributed systems that are capable of meeting the demands of today's digital landscape.

Serverless Machine Learning: Leveraging Serverless for AI/ML Workloads

Machine learning (ML) and artificial intelligence (AI) have become integral parts of modern applications, powering everything from recommendation systems to natural language processing. However, deploying and managing ML/AI workloads at scale can be challenging, requiring significant computational resources and infrastructure management. Serverless computing offers a compelling solution to these challenges by providing a scalable, cost-effective platform for deploying and running ML/AI models. In this article, we'll explore the concept of serverless machine learning, discuss its benefits, and delve into scalable software architecture patterns for building serverless systems that handle AI/ML workloads.

What is Serverless Machine Learning?

Serverless machine learning refers to the use of serverless computing platforms to deploy, manage, and scale machine learning and artificial intelligence workloads. Unlike traditional ML/AI deployment models that require provisioning and managing infrastructure, serverless machine learning abstracts away the underlying infrastructure, allowing developers to focus on building and deploying models without worrying about server management. Serverless platforms automatically scale resources based on demand, ensuring optimal performance and cost efficiency for ML/AI workloads.

Benefits of Serverless Machine Learning:

1. Scalability: Serverless platforms automatically scale resources based on workload demand, allowing ML/AI models to handle fluctuating workloads without manual intervention. This scalability is crucial for ML/AI applications that experience varying levels of traffic and computational requirements.

2. Cost Efficiency: With serverless machine learning, organizations only pay for the computational resources used during model inference, rather than for idle infrastructure. This pay-per-use pricing model can result in significant cost savings, especially for applications with unpredictable or sporadic usage patterns.

3. Reduced Management Overhead: Serverless platforms abstract away the underlying infrastructure, eliminating the need for manual provisioning, scaling, and management. This reduces the operational overhead associated with deploying and maintaining ML/AI models, allowing developers to focus on building and improving models rather than managing infrastructure.

Scalable Software Architecture Patterns for Serverless Machine Learning:

1. Model Serving with Function as a Service (FaaS):

Function as a Service (FaaS) is a serverless computing model where functions are deployed and executed in response to events. In the context of machine learning, FaaS can be used to deploy model serving functions that handle inference requests in real-time. These functions can be triggered by HTTP requests, message queues, or other event sources, allowing for seamless integration with existing applications.

Example Code (Python with AWS Lambda):

```python
import boto3
```

```
# Initialize AWS Lambda client
lambda_client = boto3.client('lambda')

# Define model serving function
def serve_model(event, context):
    # Load ML model
    model = load_model()

    # Perform inference
    input_data = event['data']
    result = model.predict(input_data)

    return result

# Deploy model serving function as a serverless function
on AWS Lambda
```
```

## 2. Asynchronous Batch Processing:

For ML/AI workloads that require batch processing of large datasets, asynchronous batch processing can be a scalable solution. In this pattern, batch processing jobs are triggered by events or scheduled at regular intervals, allowing for efficient utilization of serverless resources. Results can be stored in a data store or sent to downstream systems for further processing.
```

Example Code (Python with AWS Batch):

```python
import boto3

# Initialize AWS Batch client
batch_client = boto3.client('batch')

# Define batch processing job
def process_batch(event, context):
    # Trigger batch processing job
    job_id = batch_client.submit_job(
        jobName='batch-job',
        jobQueue='batch-queue',
        jobDefinition='batch-definition',
        parameters={
            'input_data': event['data']
        }
    )['jobId']

    return job_id

# Deploy batch processing function as a serverless function on AWS Lambda
```

3. Model Training with Managed Services:

For training ML models, managed services such as Amazon SageMaker provide serverless platforms that handle the underlying infrastructure and orchestration. Developers can leverage SageMaker's built-in algorithms and frameworks, as well as custom training scripts, to train and deploy ML models at scale. SageMaker automatically handles provisioning, scaling, and monitoring, making it an ideal choice for serverless machine learning.

Example Code (Python with Amazon SageMaker):

```python
import sagemaker

# Initialize SageMaker session and estimator
sagemaker_session = sagemaker.Session()
estimator = sagemaker.estimator.Estimator(
    image_uri='sagemaker-training-image',
    role='arn:aws:iam::123456789012:role/service-role/AmazonSageMaker-ExecutionRole-20220101',
    instance_count=1,
    instance_type='ml.m5.large',
    output_path='s3://sagemaker-output/'
)

# Define training data location
train_data = 's3://sagemaker-input/train_data.csv'
```

```
# Start model training job
estimator.fit(train_data)

# Deploy trained model as an endpoint for inference
endpoint = estimator.deploy(initial_instance_count=1, instance_type='ml.m5.large')
```

Serverless machine learning offers a scalable, cost-effective, and low-maintenance solution for deploying and managing ML/AI workloads. By leveraging serverless computing platforms and scalable software architecture patterns, organizations can build robust, efficient systems that handle ML/AI inference, batch processing, and model training with ease. Whether deploying model serving functions with FaaS, performing asynchronous batch processing, or training models with managed services like Amazon SageMaker, serverless machine learning empowers developers to focus on building intelligent applications without the overhead of infrastructure management.

Continuous Integration and Delivery (CI/CD) for Serverless Systems

Continuous Integration and Continuous Delivery (CI/CD) have revolutionized the software development lifecycle, enabling teams to automate the process of building, testing, and deploying applications. When it comes to serverless systems, CI/CD becomes even more critical due to the dynamic nature of serverless deployments. In this article, we'll explore how CI/CD practices can be applied to serverless systems, discuss their benefits, and delve into scalable software architecture patterns for building CI/CD pipelines tailored for serverless applications.

Understanding CI/CD for Serverless Systems:

CI/CD for serverless systems involves automating the deployment pipeline for serverless applications, from code commits to production deployment. The goal is to streamline the development process, reduce manual errors, and ensure that changes are deployed quickly and reliably. Key components of CI/CD for serverless systems include automated testing, version control, deployment automation, and monitoring.

Benefits of CI/CD for Serverless Systems:

1. Faster Time to Market: By automating the deployment pipeline, CI/CD reduces the time it takes to deliver new features and updates to production. This enables organizations to iterate more quickly and respond to customer feedback faster, leading to a shorter time to market.

2. Improved Reliability: CI/CD pipelines automate the process of building, testing, and deploying applications, reducing the likelihood of human error. Automated testing ensures that each change is thoroughly validated before being deployed to production, resulting in more reliable software.

3. Scalability: Serverless systems are inherently scalable, and CI/CD pipelines designed for serverless applications can easily scale to handle increased workload demands. Automated deployment and scaling mechanisms ensure that applications can seamlessly handle fluctuations in traffic and demand.

Scalable Software Architecture Patterns for CI/CD in Serverless Systems:

1. Infrastructure as Code (IaC):

Infrastructure as Code (IaC) is a practice where infrastructure is defined and managed using code. In the context of serverless systems, IaC enables teams to define the configuration of serverless resources, such as functions, APIs, and databases, using declarative code. This code is version controlled and can be automatically deployed as part of the CI/CD pipeline, ensuring consistency and reproducibility across environments.

Example Code (Terraform):

```terraform
# Define AWS Lambda function
resource "aws_lambda_function" "example" {
  function_name = "example-function"
  runtime = "python3.8"
  handler = "handler.lambda_handler"
  ...
}

# Define AWS API Gateway endpoint
resource "aws_api_gateway_rest_api" "example" {
  name = "example-api"
  ...
}

# Define API Gateway resource and method
resource "aws_api_gateway_resource" "example" {
  rest_api_id = aws_api_gateway_rest_api.example.id
  parent_id = aws_api_gateway_rest_api.example.root_resource_id
  path_part = "example"
}

resource "aws_api_gateway_method" "example" {
  rest_api_id = aws_api_gateway_rest_api.example.id
```

```
  resource_id = aws_api_gateway_resource.example.id
  http_method = "POST"
}
```

2. Automated Testing:

Automated testing is a critical component of CI/CD for serverless systems. Unit tests, integration tests, and end-to-end tests ensure that each change to the codebase is thoroughly validated before being deployed to production. In serverless environments, testing can be automated using frameworks such as AWS Lambda Test, Jest, or Pytest, which provide tools for writing and running tests for serverless functions.

Example Code (Python with Pytest):

```python
# test_handler.py
import handler

def test_lambda_handler():
    event = {...}
    context = {...}
    response = handler.lambda_handler(event, context)
    assert response == {...}
```

3. Canary Deployments:

Canary deployments involve gradually rolling out changes to a small subset of users or traffic, allowing for real-time monitoring and validation before fully deploying to production. In serverless systems, canary deployments can be implemented using features such as AWS Lambda aliases and traffic shifting, which enable controlled traffic routing to different versions of a function.

Example Code (AWS Lambda Aliases):

```bash
# Create new version of Lambda function
aws lambda create-function \
  --function-name example-function \
  --zip-file fileb://function.zip \
  --handler handler.lambda_handler \
  --runtime python3.8 \
  --role arn:aws:iam::123456789012:role/lambda-execution-role \
  --publish

# Update alias to point to new version
aws lambda update-alias \
  --function-name example-function \
```

```
  --name prod \
  --function-version 2
```

CI/CD practices are essential for ensuring the reliability, scalability, and agility of serverless systems. By automating the deployment pipeline, teams can accelerate the delivery of new features and updates while maintaining high levels of reliability and scalability. Leveraging scalable software architecture patterns such as Infrastructure as Code, automated testing, and canary deployments, organizations can build robust CI/CD pipelines tailored for serverless applications, enabling them to iterate quickly and deliver value to customers with confidence.

Conclusion

In the ever-evolving landscape of software development, embracing scalable software architecture patterns for serverless systems is paramount to staying competitive and delivering value to customers. Serverless computing has revolutionized the way we build and deploy applications, offering unparalleled scalability, cost-efficiency, and agility. By leveraging scalable architecture patterns tailored for serverless environments, organizations can unlock the full potential of serverless computing and accelerate their journey towards digital transformation.

From event-driven architectures to microservices and beyond, serverless systems offer a myriad of architectural possibilities, each uniquely suited to address specific use cases and requirements. Whether it's processing real-time data streams, serving machine learning models, or orchestrating complex workflows, serverless architecture patterns provide the flexibility and scalability needed to meet the demands of modern applications.

One of the key advantages of serverless architecture is its ability to abstract away the complexities of infrastructure management, allowing developers to focus on building and iterating on their applications rather than worrying about provisioning servers or managing scalability. With serverless computing, developers can deploy code in minutes, scale automatically to handle any workload, and pay only for the resources they use, making it an ideal platform for startups, enterprises, and everything in between.

Furthermore, serverless architecture patterns promote modularity, reusability, and composability, enabling teams to break down monolithic applications into smaller, more manageable components. This microservices approach not only enhances agility and scalability but also facilitates parallel development, enabling teams to work on different parts of the application simultaneously without stepping on each other's toes.

Additionally, serverless architecture patterns promote best practices such as Infrastructure as Code (IaC), automated testing, and continuous integration and delivery (CI/CD), which are essential for building robust, reliable, and maintainable systems. By treating infrastructure as code, organizations can ensure consistency, reproducibility, and version control across environments, streamlining the deployment process and reducing the risk of configuration drift.

Moreover, automated testing and CI/CD pipelines enable organizations to deliver software with confidence, knowing that each change has been thoroughly tested and validated before being deployed to production. Canary deployments further mitigate risk by enabling organizations to gradually roll out changes to a subset of users or traffic, allowing for real-time monitoring and validation before fully deploying to production.

In conclusion, scalable software architecture patterns for serverless systems offer a roadmap for organizations to harness the full power of serverless computing and accelerate their journey towards digital transformation. By embracing event-driven architectures, microservices, Infrastructure as Code, automated testing, and CI/CD, organizations can build resilient, scalable, and agile applications that deliver value to customers faster and more efficiently than ever before. The future of software development is serverless, and the possibilities are limitless.

Appendix

Glossary of Serverless Terms

Serverless computing has revolutionized the way we build and deploy applications, introducing a plethora of new concepts and terminology. This glossary provides a comprehensive overview of key terms related to serverless systems and scalable software architecture patterns.

1. Serverless Computing: Serverless computing is a cloud computing model where cloud providers dynamically manage the allocation and provisioning of servers, allowing developers to focus on writing code without worrying about infrastructure management.

2. Function as a Service (FaaS): Function as a Service (FaaS) is a serverless computing model where developers can deploy individual functions that are executed in response to events or triggers. FaaS platforms automatically scale resources based on demand, ensuring optimal performance and cost efficiency.

3. Event-Driven Architecture: Event-driven architecture (EDA) is a software design pattern where applications respond to events generated by external or internal sources. In serverless systems, EDA is commonly used to trigger serverless functions in response to events such as HTTP requests, database changes, or messaging queue notifications.

4. Microservices: Microservices is an architectural style where applications are composed of small, independent services that communicate via APIs. In serverless systems, microservices can be deployed as serverless functions, enabling greater flexibility, scalability, and fault isolation.

5. Infrastructure as Code (IaC): Infrastructure as Code (IaC) is a practice where infrastructure is defined and managed using code. In serverless systems, IaC enables teams to define the configuration of serverless resources, such as functions, APIs, and databases, using declarative code, which can be version controlled and automatically deployed.

6. Continuous Integration (CI): Continuous Integration (CI) is a software development practice where code changes are automatically built, tested, and integrated into a shared repository. In serverless systems, CI pipelines automate the process of building and testing serverless functions, ensuring that each change is thoroughly validated before being deployed.

7. Continuous Delivery (CD): Continuous Delivery (CD) is a software development practice where code changes are automatically deployed to production environments. In serverless systems, CD pipelines automate the process of deploying serverless functions, enabling teams to deliver new features and updates quickly and reliably.

8. Canary Deployment: Canary deployment is a deployment strategy where changes are gradually rolled out to a subset of users or traffic, allowing for real-time monitoring and validation before fully deploying to production. In serverless systems, canary deployments can be implemented using features such as function aliases and traffic shifting.

9. Scalability: Scalability refers to the ability of a system to handle increasing workload demands without sacrificing performance. In serverless systems, scalability is inherent, as cloud providers automatically scale resources based on demand, allowing applications to seamlessly handle fluctuations in traffic and demand.

10. Cost Efficiency: Cost efficiency refers to the ability of a system to optimize resource usage and minimize costs. In serverless systems, cost efficiency is achieved through pay-per-use pricing models, where organizations only pay for the computational resources they use, rather than for idle capacity.

11. Event Sources: Event sources are external or internal sources that trigger serverless functions to execute. Common event sources in serverless systems include HTTP requests, database changes, messaging queue notifications, and scheduled events.

12. Cold Start: Cold start refers to the initial delay experienced when invoking a serverless function that is not currently running. Cold starts occur when a function needs to be instantiated on demand, resulting in a longer response time for the first invocation.

13. Warm Start: Warm start refers to the scenario where a serverless function is already running and ready to handle invocations, resulting in a shorter response time compared to cold starts. Warm starts occur when a function remains idle for a period of time, allowing it to be reused for subsequent invocations.

14. Multi-Cloud Deployment: Multi-cloud deployment refers to the practice of deploying serverless functions across multiple cloud providers, reducing vendor lock-in and increasing resilience. Multi-cloud deployments can be achieved using cloud-agnostic frameworks and tools that abstract away provider-specific details.

15. Serverless Framework: The Serverless Framework is an open-source framework that simplifies the deployment and management of serverless applications. It provides a set of command-line tools and plugins for defining, deploying, and monitoring serverless functions across multiple cloud providers.

16. Observability: Observability refers to the ability to understand and monitor the behavior of a system by collecting and analyzing telemetry data. In serverless systems, observability is crucial for detecting and diagnosing issues, optimizing performance, and ensuring reliability.

17. Auto Scaling: Auto scaling is a feature provided by cloud providers that automatically adjusts the number of resources allocated to a serverless function based on demand. Auto scaling ensures that applications can handle fluctuations in traffic and demand without manual intervention.

18. Managed Services: Managed services are cloud services provided by cloud providers that abstract away the complexities of infrastructure management. In serverless systems, managed services such as AWS Lambda, Azure Functions, and Google Cloud Functions provide platforms for deploying and running serverless functions without the need to manage servers.

19. Stateless Functions: Stateless functions are serverless functions that do not maintain state between invocations. In serverless systems, stateless functions are preferred, as they can be easily scaled and managed by cloud providers without the need for persistent infrastructure.

20. Hybrid Deployment: Hybrid deployment refers to the practice of deploying serverless functions alongside traditional, on-premises infrastructure. Hybrid deployments enable organizations to leverage the benefits of serverless computing while maintaining legacy systems that cannot be easily migrated to the cloud.

In conclusion, mastering the terminology and concepts related to serverless systems and scalable software architecture patterns is essential for building robust, efficient, and scalable applications. By understanding the principles behind serverless computing, developers and organizations can harness the full potential of cloud computing and accelerate their journey towards digital transformation.

Serverless Best Practices Checklist

Serverless computing has emerged as a powerful paradigm for building scalable, cost-effective, and efficient applications. However, to fully realize the benefits of serverless, it's essential to follow best practices that ensure reliability, performance, and security. This checklist provides a comprehensive guide to serverless best practices, covering architecture, development, deployment, and operations.

1. Architecture Best Practices:

- **Use Event-Driven Architecture:** Design applications to respond to events triggered by external or internal sources. Leverage serverless functions to process events asynchronously, enabling decoupled and scalable architectures.

```python
# Example of event-driven architecture with AWS Lambda
import boto3

def event_handler(event, context):
    # Process incoming event
    data = event['data']
    # Perform computation or invoke other services
```

```
        result = process_data(data)
        return result
```

- **Embrace Microservices:** Decompose applications into small, independently deployable services. Deploy microservices as serverless functions to facilitate scalability, fault isolation, and faster development cycles.

```python
# Example of microservices architecture with AWS Lambda
def user_service(event, context):
    # Handle user-related operations
    ...

def product_service(event, context):
    # Handle product-related operations
    ...
```

- **Optimize for Stateless Execution:** Design serverless functions to be stateless, avoiding reliance on local state or external resources. Statelessness enables better scalability, fault tolerance, and simpler management.

```python
```

```
# Example of stateless function with AWS Lambda
def lambda_handler(event, context):
    # Process event without relying on external state
    result = process_event(event)
    return result
```

2. **Development Best Practices:**

- **Follow Infrastructure as Code (IaC):** Define serverless resources using code to ensure consistency, repeatability, and version control. Use tools like Terraform or AWS CloudFormation to manage infrastructure declaratively.

```terraform
# Example of defining AWS Lambda function with Terraform
resource "aws_lambda_function" "example" {
  function_name = "example-function"
  runtime = "python3.8"
  handler = "handler.lambda_handler"
  ...
}
```

- **Write Unit Tests:** Develop comprehensive unit tests for serverless functions to validate their behavior and functionality. Use testing frameworks like Pytest or Jest to automate the testing process.

```python
# Example of unit test for AWS Lambda function
def test_lambda_handler():
    event = {...}
    context = {...}
    response = lambda_handler(event, context)
    assert response == {...}
```

- **Monitor Performance:** Monitor serverless functions for performance metrics such as execution time, memory usage, and error rates. Leverage cloud provider monitoring tools or third-party solutions for real-time insights into function performance.

```python
# Example of monitoring performance with AWS CloudWatch
import boto3

def lambda_handler(event, context):
```

```
# Process event
...
# Log performance metrics
client = boto3.client('cloudwatch')
client.put_metric_data(
    Namespace='FunctionMetrics',
    MetricData=[
        {
            'MetricName': 'ExecutionTime',
            'Value': execution_time,
            'Unit': 'Milliseconds'
        },
```
```

**3. Deployment Best Practices:**

- **Implement CI/CD Pipelines:** Automate the deployment process with continuous integration and continuous delivery (CI/CD) pipelines. Use tools like AWS CodePipeline or GitHub Actions to automate building, testing, and deploying serverless functions.

- **Canary Deployments:** Gradually roll out changes to a subset of users or traffic to validate updates before fully deploying to production. Use features like AWS Lambda aliases and traffic shifting for canary deployments.
```

- **Version Control:** Manage code changes and infrastructure configurations using version control systems like Git. Maintain clear commit history, branching strategies, and release tagging for better collaboration and traceability.

4. **Operations Best Practices:**

- **Set Concurrency Limits:** Configure concurrency limits for serverless functions to control the maximum number of simultaneous executions. Set appropriate limits based on workload requirements and resource availability.

```yaml
# Example of setting concurrency limits with AWS Lambda
Resources:
  MyFunction:
    Type: AWS::Lambda::Function
    Properties:
      ...
      ReservedConcurrentExecutions: 100
```

- **Enable Monitoring and Logging:** Enable comprehensive monitoring and logging for serverless functions to detect performance issues, errors, and security threats. Utilize cloud provider monitoring services like AWS CloudWatch or third-party logging solutions.

- **Implement Security Best Practices:** Implement security measures such as least privilege access, encryption, and input validation to protect serverless functions from malicious attacks. Follow security best practices provided by cloud providers and security frameworks.

- **Optimize Cold Starts:** Minimize cold start latency by optimizing function initialization time, reducing package size, and using provisioned concurrency. Consider warming up functions with scheduled invocations or traffic simulation.

Following serverless best practices is essential for building robust, efficient, and scalable applications in the cloud. By embracing architecture patterns, development practices, deployment strategies, and operational guidelines tailored for serverless environments, organizations can leverage the full potential of serverless computing and accelerate their digital transformation journey. Use this checklist as a guide to ensure that your serverless applications are designed, developed, deployed, and operated according to best practices, leading to greater reliability, performance, and security.

www.ingramcontent.com/pod-product-compliance
Lightning Source LLC
Chambersburg PA
CBHW031604210526
45464CB00004B/1425